FAITH IN

Carlos Gomez

FAITH IN
Carlos Gomez

A MEMOIR OF

SALSA, SEX, AND

SALVATION

Samantha Dunn

AN OWL BOOK

HENRY HOLT AND COMPANY   NEW YORK

Owl Books
Henry Holt and Company, LLC
Publishers since 1866
175 Fifth Avenue
New York, New York 10010
www.henryholt.com

An Owl Book® and 🄷® are registered trademarks of
Henry Holt and Company, LLC

Library of Congress Cataloging-in-Publication Data

Dunn, Samantha.
   Faith in Carlos Gomez : a memoir of salsa, sex, and salvation /
Samantha Dunn.—1st ed.
      p.   cm.
   ISBN-13: 978-0-8050-8016-2
   ISBN-10: 0-8050-8016-3
   1. Salsa (Dance)—Social aspects—California.   2. Man-woman
relationships—California.   3. Dunn, Samantha.   I. Title.
   GV1796.S245D86 2005
   818'.5403—dc22   2004060939

Henry Holt books are available for special
promotions and premiums.
For details contact:
Director, Special Markets.

First Edition 2005

Designed by Paula Russell Szafranski

Printed in the United States of America
1 3 5 7 9 10 8 6 4 2

for Edward

FAITH IN

Carlos Gomez

Welcome to
DanceLand Academy

Salsa is an upbeat Latin dance that is easy to learn! We also teach Merengue and Cha-Cha-Cha as part of the salsa curriculum. These three dances are very popular in L.A.'s nightclub scene.

All this happens in the year I learn to speak Spanish for real, the year I start to salsa dance, the year I feel my heart break, the year I sleep with a short man from Cuba.

Salsa is mambo by any other name, some say, or perhaps its first cousin done up with a little Hustle and disco from the seventies. But this really tells you nothing about what it becomes in your body, how it infiltrates your soul, the stuff it moves around in your head, the places it takes

you, the things it makes you do. What you need to understand is that the music and the steps of the dance are living
threads that weave back through the tropics, back to the
Iberian Peninsula, and back still to the African continent,
where echoes of the same rhythms form prayer to gods so
ancient their names are not remembered. It's fair for me to
say that dancing salsa is like using a Ouija board—be careful,
because through your play you may be invoking something
more powerful than you can handle. I'm warning you now,
because nobody warned me.

This story, like many I tell, begins with my horse, Harley.
Or maybe this is not a story at all, but a line of events
tumbling against one another like dominoes. Whatever it
is, it begins on a January day in a canyon by the beach, the
kind of California day that denies the very existence of anything called winter and suspends us in a perpetual spring.
The sky cloudless, the breeze mild, the grass soft, the water
shining. Such is the stuff that makes Southern Californians
so convinced everything will always be possible.

No healthy, relatively able-bodied person should be
expected to labor on a Monday in January that's as warm as
any summer day known in Moscow, say, or Bangor, Maine.
It would be committing some degree of sin to sit in front of
a computer screen and type. I decide it is not only reasonable

but totally necessary to pull on my riding boots at three in the afternoon and drive to the stable to take my aging Thoroughbred out for a ride. He suffers from arthritis caused by his early career as a racehorse, so of course the warmth of this day and some mild exercise could be nothing but beneficial. (Not that I need this excuse to stop working. I'm the kind of woman who finds a reason most any afternoon to quit what I'm doing and go to the stable, regardless of the weather. Luckily I'm self-employed.)

As I'm putting the halter around Harley's sleek bay head, I happen to look down and notice he's missing the shoe that should form an iron crescent around his front right hoof. He'll come up lame without his shoe. There goes my afternoon ride.

"Did you get a little kooky running around the pasture this morning? Is that how you lost your shoe? Did you do it on purpose? Huh?" I'm not really expecting this interrogation to yield any confession, but I have a habit of talking to my horse, partly because he constantly twitches his muzzle and moves his lips, as if he's on the verge of speech. Being Harley's owner is like going out with a star-quarterback, red-Camaro-driving boyfriend; it always seems that he's about to say something really interesting, but, somehow, that never quite materializes.

Harley gets a carrot and a kiss on the forehead before I go to the barn to phone my farrier, which is the equestrian's way to say horseshoer or blacksmith. If, upon reading the word *blacksmith,* an image pops to mind of a muscled, broad-backed, dark-haired man stripped to the waist, wet with the sweat of hard labor and heat from a forge, that image would be the correct image in this case. Let's call him Rafael, which is nowhere near his real name, and let's say he's from Argentina, which he's not. A rich accent with rolling *r*'s and wide vowels flavors his speech; even his fluent English has a flow and lull, a rhythm not unlike the sound of the Pecos River running over rocks. He smiles easily; he sings songs in Spanish under his breath as he works. Animals love him.

All this I haven't avoided noticing over the course of the eight years he's been my farrier. Every six weeks, when it's time for Harley's new shoes, we meet at the barn to trade bad jokes and barn gossip. Usually we continue the conversation with lunch at Coogies, the Denny's of Malibu. We have shared divorce stories and attorney's numbers. (We know the childhood dreams of what we each wanted to be; he, a guitar player, I, a veterinarian.) He has put his arm around my shoulders when I have been too depressed to lift my head, and he has seen me bandaged and shrunken days after a riding accident with Harley that nearly left me an amputee. That accident was of such a magnitude that it created a new center of gravity for me, becoming the navigation point for the rest of my life. Among the many lessons I took from that experience was that there are people who can tolerate illness and injury, and those who can't. Rafael is one who can. He was one of the first visitors I had the day I returned home from my longest stay in the hospital. He even felt a measure of ill-placed guilt, because during my accident I was trampled under the sharp metal of the new shoes he'd put on Harley the day before, which carved through my left leg, leaving it attached by sinew only inches wide.

The logical question here would be, my God, girl, what kept you from being swept off your feet all these years by this horsewoman's Adonis? Or pulling him into the hayloft and making merry? A few factors have been at work. One: few barns in Southern California are built with actual haylofts. Two: we have both been committed to other people at various times. Three: far from being a femme fatale, I easily fall into the role of what has been termed a *guy's gal,* as in one of the guys, as in tell-her-your-problems, gee-you're-a-great-pal-and-it's-just-a-bonus-that-you've-got-big-boobs, let's-watch-the-Tyson-fight-on-pay-per-view kind of woman. I don't usually inspire men to romance.

But on this day in January, Rafael picks up the phone, and I say, hey, Raf, it's Sam, Harley threw a shoe. And he says, shit, well, anyways don't worry, he's almost due so I'll stop by late morning tomorrow. Then he says, I'll call you before I get there so maybe we can have lunch like always, and I say, let me give you my new phone number. At that he asks, new phone number?—puzzlement in his tone—and I reply, yeah, I moved out of the apartment in Santa Monica a while ago.

"What's that mean? You and that guy broke up after all?"

"We did indeed. It was a long time coming." (Here's where I might sigh.)

"That's great. I mean, too bad," he says, not sounding at all sympathetic that yet another long-term relationship of mine has withered and died, the one after my divorce, the one nobody but me thought would end happily ever after.

"Well, so," he's saying, "what're you doing for dinner tonight?"

And that's how he ends up pulling into the driveway to take me to an Italian restaurant, the two of us both single at the same time for the first time. I'll freeze the frame of him getting out of the little sporty car: His hair shines so black it makes the black of the T-shirt stretched across his chest seem faded. His jeans are in fact faded, but his boots, they're polished. He wears two shiny silver rings on his right hand, one on the thumb and the other on the middle finger. He says, *Hola guapa,* and while it's nice to be called beautiful by any-one at any time, it sounds even better when an Argentinean farrier says it in his native language, like it spontaneously occurred to him at the sight of you, like the reaction was so immediate he didn't have time to think of the English word. By way of hello he kisses me not on the cheek per usual but square on the mouth. He tastes faintly of tobacco and red wine; his lips are edged with a light stubble.

We don't make it to dinner that night. We make it to breakfast the next day. Imagine eight years of sexual tension, finally released. I can't do anything that morning but drink coffee with one hand. If I smoked, I'd have held a cigarette in the other.

Immediately I fall, as my family's expression goes, ass-over-teacup for Rafael. I have never felt such an intense craving for the physical presence of a man, ever (except perhaps that semester in high school when I had a crush on John Lucero from biology class and for three weeks dotted my *i*'s with little hearts). A type of delirium takes hold of me. I fall asleep in Rafael's blacksmith arms as he reads Isabelle Allende stories out loud to me the way they were written, not in translation. Then there are the phone calls in the middle of the day telling me what he's thinking (something to do with a certain mole on my body, but I will go no farther here), the kissing until the skin on my lips rubs off, the ice cream (enough about the ice cream).

Anything not directly involved in making love with Rafael becomes difficult. Work, for example. Eating too. My ability to concentrate seems to evaporate like steam. A Greek chorus of girlfriends fills my ears:

"This guy has a black belt in romance," says Bev.

"You don't stand a chance against this," says J.

"Are you making him up? No guy is this hot," says Rachel.

"Oh no, those Argentines. Watch out," says Tina.

February comes, and with it Valentine's Day.

Rafael says, "Why don't you come over, and I'll make dinner."

Pedicure, body buffing, waxing of eyebrows and every other conceivable area of the body, strategic perfume placement—it all takes time. I get up at seven in the morning so I'll be ready for our date by seven that night.

The cabernet and vanilla candles are in place when I arrive at his house. He's cooking, but I am sitting at the kitchen table chopping the onions, and while I do this he says he'll be right back, that we need some music.

The room soon fills with a tide of drums and a thumping bass that causes my shoulders to move as if possessed by a spirit not my own. A man's deep voice seems to call across a jungle, the brass of trumpets like bird sounds in the night.

"Put the knife down," he says, extending a hand to me. "I want to show you how we dance salsa."

"Oh, no no no. Me white girl, no dance." I wave the knife in punctuation of my point.

"It's easy," he says as he takes the knife away. "I'll show you."

I can recite a litany of valid reasons why this dancing thing is a bad idea, but I don't think I'll need to do more than point to my bum left leg, which he knows still swells and suffers shooting pain at unpredictable moments. A titanium rod runs the length of my shin bone, a thick scar cuts the circumference of my calf midway down, and a fist-sized dent in the muscle points to the spot where surgeons sewed everything back together.

"Come on, you ride all the time, you do yoga. You went rock climbing a couple months ago." He's pulling me to my feet.

True, all true. At this point in my life I've managed to land a regular freelance job reporting West Coast health and fitness trends for a New York magazine, a post that forces me to attend all manner of exercise-related events, me the stand-in for "every woman," the idea being that if I can do it, most anybody can.

I try another tack, namely, that he knows I'm a klutz to a near pathological degree, so much so I wrote an entire book about it, and that although I no longer suffer accidents on a regular basis, I am still gawky and fumbling in my manner. What's more, I am a child of rock and roll, and I do mean the hard stuff.

"You know I was a headbanger, Raf," I protest. "I'm talking heavy metal, grunge, mosh pits."

"It's OK, it's only the two of us here." He smiles (even, snow-colored teeth, pleasing as a picket fence).

I don't get to explain to him the part about my mother being a dancer, or should I say danced in one of her many professions before nursing school. As a child she began with ballet, grew and learned the jitterbug, the waltz, Lindy Hop, samba—I don't even have names for moves she could once make with her feet. She worked briefly as a ballroom instructor at an Arthur Murray Dance Studio in one of the rusting towns of western Pennsylvania and then later, in the air force, did rumba exhibitions at the officers' club with a friend of hers named Rick. She met my father dancing. Supposedly it is the one thing they had in common, their love of dancing. Since he spoke Italian and she English, conversation was out. Or so I imagine. Can't say for sure. I never met him. At any rate, by the time I was a teenager, my mother, grandmother, and I were living in the remote northern New Mexico town of Las Vegas, and every once in a while I'd hear her humming a song when she came home late from bars like El Rialto or Los Dos Indios. The scent of her drugstore perfume hung in the hall, and I knew she had been dancing. Growing up, I considered social dancing to be something my mother did, and anything my mother did was categorically uncool and therefore could not, did not, would not interest me, ever.

But I don't get to explain any of this because Ruben has already pulled me into his arms, our bare feet growing cold on the linoleum. He shows me a rhythm that goes quick-quick-slow, quick-quick-slow, and I step all over his toes. I move forward when I should move back, bumping his chin. It doesn't seem to matter. I feel exquisite in his arms. We kiss and kiss and make use of the kitchen counter and end up burning the tuna steaks.

Later that night, Rafael says sometime I should get my girlfriends together. He says, "I'll get Manuel and Javier to come out so we can all go dancing."

"When?" I try to sound casual.

"Probably next Saturday," he murmurs as he pulls the bed covers around him.

Today is Friday, so that means I have a week, seven slim days, to learn to dance. I can't sleep imagining the humiliation of me on a dance floor, all wooden-limbed like a dumb puppet next to these gorgeous, slinky men, and them looking at me and then at Rafael, thinking, *What's he see in her?* Then I imagine Rafael shaking his head in disappointment, thinking, *What did I see in her?* and all the red-roses-and-champagne thoughts that have seized him suddenly dissipate with the image of me dancing. All right, OK, I know this is the kind of stupid logic you only suffer during an infatuation, but right then I'm near drowning in infatuation. I'm thinking, *So what if we don't have anything other than horses in common? Surely this degree of lust must be destined to blossom into something profound.* They make movies about this exact scenario: two friends finally sleep together and realize what they've been looking for has been under their noses the entire time. Right?

Right?

That night I outline a plan to pitch a magazine assignment, some salsa-as-exercise trend. This way, unbeknownst to Rafael, I'll be able to take a couple of private lessons, so that when we hit the dance floor, Cupid will land a bull's-eye straight through his heart.

Only, it doesn't work out that way.

Salsa 7

You may start Beginning Salsa at anytime! Our Salsa program does not run in sessions, and no partner is required. The basic and side basic (cumbia) steps are acquired here:

To sing you must first open your mouth, the writer Henry Miller once observed. He might have added the corollary, to dance you must take the first step.

Five queries to dance studios and dance shoe shops yield two possibilities for private instructors: the first is a guy called Ken, and the second has a name elaborate as lace, screaming a history of conquistadores and red tile, mournful guitars, mantillas, sangria, bullfights, and death in the afternoon. I follow my bias toward cultural authenticity and make the call.

He picks up on the first ring, a fact I will later come to see as a portent of fate. He rarely picks up any call on the first ring, waiting instead to see the number on the phone's caller ID before deciding to answer or not.

I begin with a blah-blah-blah about being some kind of journalist who needs to have a dance lesson in order to write a story. I'm using my professional voice—crisp articulation, half an octave below my everyday voice—that makes me sound more impressive. But he's silent on the other end, none of the usual "oh, reallys" and "wow that's great" the professional voice so often elicits. I grow nervous, press the receiver more tightly to my ear. What if he says no?

I break down.

"Listen, I have to tell you the truth." I'm honestly pleading in my everyday voice. "The deal is I'm nuts over a guy from South America, and I have to have a lesson so I can dance with him and make him fall in love with me. But I'll do some reporting too; I'm not making that part up. And I'll pay you whatever you want." I don't care if I have to skip a car payment in order to pay, I'm getting a lesson.

A hesitation on the line. I think I hear him exhale.

"I tell you what," he says at last. "Tomorrow is my birthday, but since it's for true love, I'll come in just to teach you."

"Really? You'd do that? Really?" This is a squeal.

"It will be my pleasure," he says in a courtly manner, and I imagine him a tall, thin, middle-aged gentleman from the Old Country, someplace where they still remember the codes surrounding romance, where science and psycho-analysis have yet to strip the varnish off the search for love. I'm figuring that in one hour he will relieve me from my total ignorance of this mystery called dance, thus by extension ensure my success in establishing a significant, lasting partnership with a living being other than my horse.

The seventy-five-dollar rate for a private lesson even strikes me as incredibly reasonable. Granted, I stopped going to therapy because the same rate for a shrink was too steep for my budget (if it can be said that I maintain any kind of a budget, ever). But, come on, this is about priorities. Romance versus mental health—what's going to win out? Everybody knows the answer. The page in my agenda book for that day reads:

✔ 5:15 p.m. *Dance Lesson!*

This quest has led to a place where I would otherwise never be caught, living or dead. A street-side dance studio, specifically, where huge windows put the sight of average people attempting to capture rhythm on display to the passing traffic. Imagine. Give it a minute and let the abject horror of that picture really sink in.

I'm wearing sneakers, dressed as I would be for the gym, not having had even the most remote guess regarding what the appropriate attire is for a dance lesson. I stand in the middle of a floor that must be made of wood yet reflects light more like glass. A big disco—disco!—ball hangs in the center of the low ceiling, mirrors line the walls, and a chrome-and-Formica table-and-chair set occupies one corner of the large room. A Benny Goodman tune over the speakers competes with the sound coming off a video monitor playing an endless loop of couples in a ballroom competition, a cheery voice-over chirping something to do with a video series transforming Quasimodo and Esmeralda into Fred and Ginger. Or that's my interpretation. In the air I perceive an odor that I will come to know as the product of sweat and synthetic fiber, tinged with a suggestion of cologne. It smells, strangely, rather pleasant. Yet the collective impression is, how do I say, dorky. Goofy. Out. Lame. Over. And there's an indefinable element I can't put my finger on, akin to a seventies-porn quality, all chest hair and frosted highlights, vinyl couch and Baldwin Fun Machine.

But another part of me knows that good lessons can come from anywhere, me, who after fifteen years of living in L.A. has learned to breathe out of her left nostril and concentrate on a third eye and sit folded in a lotus position. Never thought I would be doing any of that, either. I don't know why it has any effect, but it does, and has proved useful in making me not quite so much of a lunatic.

I am wondering where my instructor is. A few men stand in the room as if waiting for someone, but they don't seem to fit the name. They're dressed in khaki pants or slacks of some sort or other; they look like they could be teaching golf. They appear, in a word, *sensible*. Sensible is acceptable, perhaps even desirable, for the waltz or fox-trot but is not what I had in mind for learning Latin dancing. At this time, yes, I am still gaga over Rafael. Even so, any woman secretly wishes that her Latin dance teacher be dashing, faintly exotic, a version of the silver-screen Valentino. A gay Valentino most desired of all (that is to say sexy, without the complications of sexy).

Then I hear, "Are you Samantha?" and notice for the first time a man standing in front of me, smiling. Wavy hair shining like wet obsidian. Neatly pressed gray pants, a striped shirt with a cord that picks up the precise shade of gray. Shoes buffed to military standards. Lithe physique, even features. I see faint scars from battles with a once-bad complexion and a thin, jagged white line at the eyebrow, implying it was once cut open violently, maybe by a fist or a broken bottle. The man is impeccable, elegant, but suggesting the flavor of danger. This is a Latin dance teacher to end all others, a dream of central casting.

Except.

The top of his head reaches up to my armpit.

That's not totally accurate. His head actually hits just under my chin, putting his face in line with the center of my chest. And he is not an old, courtly gentleman but a young man, younger than the neat, conservative attire suggests.

"Yes! Hi! I'm Samantha! Please call me Sam!" I know! I'm speaking! In exclamations! The product of feeling strangely relieved and disappointed all at once. I continue with this weirdly excited speech as I detail all the reasons why even the lowest expectations of me as a student will not be exceeded, how I have no ability, why I have a titanium leg, that I am far more comfortable walking through horseshit than I am stepping onto a dance floor. He's silent, nodding his head, an earnest expression aimed at me for the five minutes it takes to complete my monologue.

"Do you feel better now?" he says when at last I finish.

"Yes?" I venture, unsure of the reason for the question.

"That's great," he says. "Everybody says some version of what you just told me when they start. But if you can walk, you can learn to dance, OK? Believe me. Now let's dance."

Walking is not so easy, I want to say. I want to say that it took me a good two years after my accident to walk without a limp, but he is holding my hand and turning me toward the mirrored wall. The grip of his fingers indicates strength, but the skin is smooth, the skin of a life lived mostly indoors, and I am at once aware of my own fingers, callused from holding rope and reins, nails broken, an angry hangnail reddening my thumb.

"When I say 'one,' step back with your right foot. OK? One."

I step, then look to his reflection for approval. Standing next to him I picture myself in a horned helmet and yellow

braids, all the hulking femaleness of a German opera heroine. He, so contained and slender, a leather whip of a man,
somewhat cruel in an oddly appealing way.

"Very good. Let's review. One." His expression, deadpan.

I step back again, but I step with the left foot.

"Let's try it with your *other* left. Yes, that means your
right."

"See what I mean?" I tell him, my hands shooting up
in a gesture of I-told-you-so. "I've never been accused of
coordination."

"Ssssh." He puts a finger to his lips, then points to me in
the mirror. "Forget all that. Just move your right foot back
when I say 'one.' Easy. No problem. One."

I do. I manage to distinguish left from right and actually move the correct foot.

"Beautiful." Pronouncing the word with a long stress
in the middle, so it becomes *bew-teeeee-fil,* he permits a
slight crease at the corner of his lips, the dawn of what will
be a smile. "Would you look at that. You're dancing. Now
let's do that five hundred more times."

We both laugh, and right then I feel something loosen,
the grip of nervousness around my throat, the pinch of
tension in my jaw.

He's kidding only a little. We do repeat that single
movement in the mirror for several minutes before he allows
me to try the next step, which is only to move my left foot
in a small motion in place. "One-two," he says over and

over, "One-two." On the count of three I get to move my right foot again so that I come into the same standing position as when I started.

"Very nice," he says, the tone of a teacher in a kindergarten class. "Now we're going to put those three steps together, and you're going to hold on the fourth count. That means you're not going to move. You're not going to step at all."

"Nada." I nod.

"Nothing."

"Nope. Got it."

"Good," he says. "One-two-three-*hold four.*"

Three steps and stillness. Success! I have mastered the dance. "I like the not-moving part," I tell him.

"I thought you might," he says.

Forty-five minutes later, he turns to me. The moment has come for him to explain the "closed dance position," for him to put his arm at my back, for me to place my hand on the curve of his shoulder, for us to clasp the palms of our other hands together, for . . . his nose to hit my cleavage.

Giggles rise in me with a force wholly inappropriate, like bubbles bursting from champagne uncorked. *Say something, anything, everything—he'll know why you're laughing, and his expression is so serious, so professional.* I blurt out, "Where you from?"

"Cuba."

"Havana?" I ask, it being the only city in Cuba I can readily name.

"Cienfuegos," he says, and I nod my head as if I know where the hell Cienfuegos is, and he adds, "but I was raised in New York." (I'm making this part up. The family history is much more complicated—there's a thing about his dad and Puerto Rico and New Jersey—but let's not bother with details here. As for New York—that's close enough to pass for the truth.)

From out of my mouth shoot further questions aimed at killing the giggles that might erupt at any moment, particularly now that I catch the reflection of big me paired with little him.

1. Where in New York? (*The outer boroughs.*)
2. When did you learn to dance? (*Always danced.*)
3. Who taught you? (*I'm Cuban, c'mon, learned on my own, then trained as an instructor at Arthur Murray.*)
4. What did you study in college? (*How did you know I went to college? Music theory was my major.*)
5. Why did you become a professional dancer? (*I wasn't doing anything else, and somebody said I'd be good at it.*)
6. How old are you? (*Thirty-one, today.*)

"That's right, I forgot. Happy birthday," I say, meaning it. "Thanks for making time for me."

For just a moment he looks up into my face as if he is searching for something that might be found there. "No problem. Anything I can do for true love," he says, the words holding no obvious taint of sarcasm. And then he counts "one," and in the time it takes to exhale the two of us move together. Three steps backward, three steps forward. So simple, and such an impossible accomplishment. It's taken one full hour to arrive at this point. I feel flushed and giddy.

"See, what'd I tell you? You're dancing. Next time we'll even try it with music," he says. "I mean, if you want another lesson—"

"Next week is perfect," I reply instantly. I don't know what I'm thinking, really. That it was good exercise, that I had fun, that I will dictate the fate of my romance with Rafael with one more lesson to my credit, that for one sliver of an instant not only did I not feel inept, but I experienced an unfamiliar lightness.

As it happens, before this introduction to salsa I had started taking a Spanish class at the university where I sometimes lead a writing workshop. The pay's not much, but for every class you teach, the school allows you to enroll as a student in another area of study (academia's version of a barter economy). Why I took Spanish? It was there, it was free, it was something to do in the evenings now that I was single, but, most of all, it had grown ridiculous for me to speak improperly a language I have been around most of my life, first as a child in New Mexico, then as an adult in California. That I could read Baudelaire in French but could not decipher signs in the storefronts along Pico Boulevard in the city where I live had become an irony too uncomfortable not to reconcile.

Little did I realize my Spanish lessons would prove so immediately useful. Case in point: I'm at Rafael's house just days before the big dancing date we had planned. In the morning I awake to hear him talking to someone on the phone. The tone is what first perks my interest, the same tone he uses to soothe nervous horses, to earn their confidence before he goes near their dangerous hooves, the same tone, come to think of it, he had used to invite me to the Italian restaurant.

So I listen a little more closely and pick up several interesting words: *querida*, which means "darling"; *esta noche*, meaning "tonight"; *comeremos en casa*, "we'll eat at the house." Now he could be talking to his beloved cousin, but since she still lives in Argentina, I doubt it.

Mastering language becomes a question of nuance. This turns out to be a particularly useful tutorial in the possible usages of *te quiero* and *te amo*. All my life I thought they meant the same thing, "I love you, I care for you," but they resonate very differently in context. *Querer* is the verb meaning "to want," or "to love" in the sense of prefer.

Evidently, when a man says *te quiero* to his mother or sister, it signifies love. When he says it to you while you're on your back clutching the sides of his bed, it just means "I want you," in the carnal sense. *Te amo* means "I love you," and, outside of love songs, is rarely uttered. (Interestingly enough, the word *amor*, when used as a noun, appears to be something many men of Latin heritage—regardless of their country of origin—throw around willy-nilly, as in "*Ay, mi amor, qué rico,*" but let's not get into that yet.)

This is the horrible burden of knowledge, the apple eaten; were I to have remained more ignorant of his mother tongue, I might be telling a very different tale. As it is, suddenly the doors of perception are cleansed, and I look around the room as if seeing it for the first time: the burgundy sheets, the nightstand stocked with condoms, the one well-worn Isabelle Allende novel. My eyes focus on Rafael's back, which, I can see in the morning's clear light, is covered with scratch marks that had to have been drawn from nails too long and sharp to be my own, as if he's been wrestling cougars in his spare time.

This is not a bedroom; it's the proverbial den of iniquity.

I feel a sensation in my stomach that can only be described as nausea, the feeling you get when you've eaten something rancid, or are falling down a well, or have been duped.

Naturally, I do then what any woman in my family would do at such a moment of clarity: I kick him really hard under the covers.

Since I know Rafael and how much he likes women, it should not surprise me to learn that I am only one of many, many others dancing in his kitchen, but it does, and so I cry about that over the phone to my girlfriends for a while and skip the dance lesson I had scheduled. And I decide to forget romance. Sex is one thing—like a good workout, I wholeheartedly recommend it for optimal health. However, romance doesn't suit me. Never has. Like the color pink and ruffled skirts, I just look silly in it.

Yet I cannot forget how I felt that first night in the kitchen, or how the dance instructor had made the movements look so effortless, like breathing. So when that dance instructor calls me to see if I want to schedule another lesson, I say yes. Somehow I must have known it was my chance at grace.

Private lessons are one of the best ways to learn to dance!

Unlike a group class, you get the undivided attention of your instructor. Discount packages are available. See the front desk for details!

The thing about me is that while I'm often mistaken for being gregarious, while I can be good with people, in reality I am reclusive by nature. Or perhaps not actually reclusive, but grown afraid, more rightly said, afraid of the complications being close to another person always brings and how I will surely fail to maneuver through those complications successfully. The modern world in general can do that to you.

For a long while now I have felt like I'm floating on top of life. I hold this image of being hunkered down on a little iceberg drifting over a great blueness. Below me fish, seals, penguins, whales—entire societies of species exist, engaged in the mess of life. On the horizon the outline of a continent suggests itself, land where humans make families, land where the wolves and the bears and the rabbits are living and dying in their animal ways.

But here on my iceberg, I have a meager tin pot over a small fire, which never seems to get bigger or warmer but likewise does not extinguish. It turns out that not much is actually needed to stay alive, and so I continue to go on in this way for days that grow into weeks that grow into years. I sometimes think about jumping into the water to join the life below, but I do not have the lungs or the skin for that environment; I am not of that world. There seems no way to move toward the continent where other land mammals live. For as long as I can recall I have been clinging to the idea that I would somehow just drift toward it, that through the natural flow I would, at some point, be deposited there, but I have come to realize that isn't probable.

At this point in my life, when I begin my dance lessons, I'm renting for next to nothing two lovely rooms above the driveway of a rambling old mansion in the Pacific Palisades, home to a friend's very aged father, where he lives with Nacha, the equally aged housekeeper who has been with the family for sixty years, and a revolving staff of home health-care workers. The world here is quiet and exquisite and still, a Shangri-la under glass, where it is possible to pass hours watching the process of a pink rose blossom in the garden. Such quietude suits me fine. In the past five years I have lost a marriage, all my money, and one live-in boyfriend, the two of us staying together long after we should have amicably said good-bye, like guests not understanding the party's over. The actual material sum of my life is composed of a banged-up mini sports utility vehicle, many books, a random assortment of CDs, a stereo, a television with no remote control, a blue box that contains family photos, some clothes, two computers, a printer, some costume jewelry, an expensive saddle and bridle, a leash, a camelback chair, three framed prints, and two oriental rugs.

It's not that I feel there should be more. I actually hold hard to the belief that the value of our lives is not gauged in the amount of space we take up. But value is, possibly, measured by how we connect within this web of existence. The fact that I am steward to a horse and a big dog, and daughter to my mother, constitutes the anchor of my life. Beyond that, there are a great number of friendly acquaintances who blow in and out, a few very close friends, and far beyond that, distant relatives in Seattle and on the East Coast I know largely as voices over the phone. That's pretty much it. My entire thirties have been dominated by the sense that, thread by thread, my place within this web is un-raveling, so that now I find myself feeling tethered lightly enough to society for even a mild breeze to rend me entirely away.

How to generate new connections has been the problem to solve. I experiment with different things, thinking, *Will this hook me in? Will that?* But everything seems provisional, maintained only through my ability to attend, to interact, and I have to admit that I am lazy and self-indulgent by nature. After a while it just feels like too much energy expenditure to drive somewhere to meet whomever, too much energy to think of what to say in polite conversation, too much energy to generate interest when I really have none—and then if I do, the payoff never appears commensurate with the investment, which is to say, I don't feel that much more connected than before. So, mostly, when I'm not working I would rather go riding, or practice yoga, or perhaps listen to music or read, or just sleep.

This is a roundabout explanation of why I cancel that next dance lesson and then forget to show up for another the following day. The instructor calls me several times before I finally pick up the phone, full of apologies for my rudeness and a promise to pay him for the lesson I missed, time he could have used to earn money teaching someone who really has a desire to learn. His only reply: "I've got a space this afternoon. Why don't you come by at three o'clock."

"What happened?" Today he's wearing stylish, loose jeans and a granite-colored baseball jersey, making him appear incredibly boyish, nearly adolescent. I feel a strong urge to muss his hair as I would a little boy's, but stop myself in time to avoid embarrassing us both. "You didn't seem like a flake, so I was surprised when you didn't show."

I start to invent a good excuse, then abruptly stop myself. What's the point? "Rafael wasn't what I thought," I confess, feeling foolish. The embarrassment is far worse for me than the actual loss of this lover.

He shrugs. "Fuck that guy."

"Excuse me?" I'm normally the one to use the vernacular of a longshoreman; up to this point I've yet to hear him swear.

"Fuck him. You don't need a reason to dance." All business now, he places his hands on me in the closed position. It occurs to me that apart from quick hugs I sometimes receive from male friends, a man never comes this close or touches me with such intimacy. Unless, of course, we've already slept together.

The dance studio is empty; sun coming through the large windows reflects off the disco ball, scattering light like confetti onto the floor. Today I notice the lean muscling of his arms. He would have made a good jockey. "Can you ride a horse?"

"What?"

"Just making conversation."

"Why did you ask me that?" He tilts his head to the side, questioning.

"Was that weird?"

"A little," he says.

It's quickly evident he has to teach me the essential elements of one-two-three-*hold four* all over again. I have a total lack of instinct for this rhythm, an observation I make out loud that he does not dispute. I find myself envying the deaf in their ability to feel vibrations, to experience sound waves as a natural part of the body.

"Better," he says, breaking our contact. "Think about keeping your movements small. This dance comes from slaves. First there's African music. The drums are big, right? The sounds are big. That's music from a free people. In the Caribbean the Africans were slaves. They couldn't safely express themselves. Because of that the rhythms get tighter. And the slaves moved in chains, so their steps had to be close together, but the feeling is, you know, like they wanted to be free. The dance is contained but has power. Look."

He points us toward the mirror so I can see the fullness of his movement. Elbows cocked slightly, hands at waist level, he begins to move his feet, the treading of his steps bearing no resemblance to the Frankensteinian bulk of my own. As I watch him I think of a baby python I once held at a pet store, the hypnotic coil and slide of muscle under that cool, dry hide.

"Do it with me," he orders. "Think small, small, small."

So I try to sink into the feeling, hold my body tight while moving my feet. What I don't know yet is that this dance is a practice of empathy; it demands you inhabit the history of another, forcing into you a kind of knowing that transcends all intellectual understanding. Through this I will come to realize the extent to which I career around with an openness, a largeness inherited from a people who have never questioned the right to move so.

It's likely gorillas could be taught to move their feet in the basic salsa pattern, so just memorizing "right-left-right/left-right-left" has little to do with actually dancing the mambo. Eventually you learn hand patterns— "the cuddle," "stop-and-go," "the copa" (who names these things, I have no idea)—that can seem as intricate as embroidery. These too have precisely fuck-all to do with a good dance. Mambo is about *sabor,* which literally means "flavor," but is used to describe a potent essence as impalpable as desire yet just as powerful. When the mambo is danced correctly, a particular feeling is generated, akin to, but not exactly like, the excruciating excitement of being a hair's breadth away from a person you want to kiss but haven't yet and know you shouldn't, or maybe like that twitter of fear and delight that comes in the moment right before you confess the words *I love you.*

But before I can reach any of this understanding, I have to make it through the current lesson.

"You'll get it," he reassures. "Keep going."

I do keep going. For all my mincing steps and swaying hips, I'm doing a fine impersonation of a circus bear.

"OK, stop," he says. He tries the analytical approach, explaining that salsa is merely a six-step dance on an eight-count beat driven by two sticks called claves, a sort of metronome for the fundamental rhythm that creates salsa. Then he goes to the studio's music console and begins to play a rhythm that goes tack-tack-tack (pause) tack-tack. "Hear that? Now, step one—"

I hear it. However, this doesn't help me at all.

He stands beside me and grabs my hand, the pressure firm as if he is trying to transfuse knowledge from his body into mine. "Do what I do," he says, and I attempt to. It seems a hundred minuscule maneuvers, all perfectly synchronized, create the seamless flow of his movement: the toe-first placement of his foot as his weight shifts from one leg to the other; the "contrabody motion," a circular movement of his arms in opposition to his legs (like the movement of your limbs while walking, but with finesse); the side-to-side glide of his rib cage, as if a detached, floating entity not linked to his hips or shoulders.

When he finally signals that we're done, my T-shirt lies wet against my skin like a layer of wallpaper, but I feel that I've accomplished something. What exactly, I don't know.

Of course I sign up for another lesson. One or two more and I'll understand this stuff. I've almost got it.

What became the mambo, and later salsa, is a series of movements originally concocted of a Cuban country dance called *són*, a formal Spanish dance known as *Danzón*, and *merengue* from the Dominican Republic, with seasoning from *cumbia*, *rumba*, *guaracha*, *guaguanco*. Beautiful words describing even more beautiful motions. In New York in the forties, Puerto Ricans and Cubans, rubbing shoulders with jazz musicians both black and white, mixed it all together. The word *salsa* is the perfect description, as it means "sauce," a combination of flavors that can cover a variety of things. Some aficionados draw a distinction between salsa, the music, and mambo, the dance done to the music. Others say the variations now performed are enough to make modern salsa a separate dance from mambo. I say it's all a product of a diaspora, first of the people who came from Europe and Africa to the Caribbean, then the children of that diaspora who created their own diaspora when they left the warmth of those islands for the cold of New York. It is a rhythm created from a people who have been displaced many times, which means that through this thing called salsa there is transmitted a quality of yearning, of longing for what was but no longer is, or for what cannot ever be.

But if you're like my mother, you're not interested in a dissertation on the origins of salsa right now. You're still wondering what happened after I kicked Rafael under the covers.

"What're you going to do?" she asks on one of her daily phone calls from southern New Mexico.

"I'm not going to see him again. Ever. After all his 'I think I'm falling in love with you,' 'you're the most amazing woman I've ever known' crap. I got up that morning, pulled my jeans on, and said, 'Good-bye.' I erased his e-mail from the computer. And I even deleted his number from my cell phone." If a man's number is deleted from my cell phone directory, he has, for all practical purposes, ceased to exist. It's my own private voodoo for banishing those who cause me pain and upset.

"No, I mean about Harley," she says.

Any horsewoman knows it's harder to find a good farrier than a good lover. Hence the reason it's never a wise idea to sleep with yours, lest unsolvable emotional entanglements interfere with your horse's ultimate comfort and performance.

"Of course he'll still shoe Harley," I reassure her. "I'm just going to leave a check at the barn when he's due."

"Smart," she says. "Too bad about Raf, though. On a scale of one to ten, he was an eleven."

"Thanks for reminding me."

"A real fox."

"Jesus, Mom, nobody says 'fox' anymore, that was already passé by the time I was in high school." I'm growing irritated, as I so often do, with her particular brand of maternal comfort.

"I still think he was a fox——" The sentence is cut short by a series of hacking coughs, not unlike the sound of an old car's muffler. It's ten in the morning, meaning she's probably only on her third cigarette before lunch.

I wait a second for quiet to return to the line. "You OK?"

"Sure," she says on the inhale. "But I mean, holy shit, he was a real hunk."

My only hope is to change the subject, so I tell her I've taken a few dance lessons.

"*You?* Oh, I'd pay money to see that," she says. "Just don't break your instructor's toes. Your mother was a dance instructor, you know."

"And a cocktail waitress and a magazine subscription salesgirl and an air traffic controller in the air force. I know, Mom." The problem with modern telephones is that there is no cord to wrap between your fingers to idle away the minutes.

"Yeah, but I was a really good dancer." Puff. Puff. "Shitty waitress. God, was I one shitty waitress. And I was a rotten instructor with a capital *R*. You know how I am. I tell you once, I tell you again, then on the third time I want to kill you dead."

Just when I think we're done, she surprises me with "Well, keep it up, honey. Dancing's in your blood, after all. You might be good at it."

"It appears to be a recessive gene." Yet I feel warm, which tells me I'm happy.

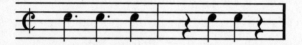

This is about the fourth lesson, and I can't even remember the basic steps from one week to the next. The instructor is again explaining something he calls the "cross-body lead," which seems to involve me taking three steps forward, then turning to the left or right; I'm not quite getting it, am instead wondering if I'll have time to oil my saddle this evening, and if my editors are going to want revisions on the article I turned in today, and if the check will get to me in time to make my quarterly tax payment, and—

With his right hand he shakes my rib cage none too gently. He's looking up at me, mouth set in a straight line. "Vexed" is the word that best applies.

"I know you want to learn this because you're here and you keep showing up, but you're not giving me anything to work with." He increases the pressure of his hands against my back and my palm. "Look alive. Come on."

I try to feel contrite yet am instantly besieged by an image from the movie *Dirty Dancing*, where the instructor likewise scolds the frivolous girl. Picture our real-time scene, where

I have the proportions of Patrick Swayze and he of Jennifer Grey. This time I really do start laughing.

"What's so funny?"

"Just that this is like that scene from *Dirty Dancing,* you know—"

"Right, just like it," he says, a smile starting to form. "Except we haven't slept together." Pause. "Yet."

Did he really just say "slept together yet"? *Yet?* Surely he didn't intend to imply, you know, I mean, that's absurd. I look down at this short man who holds me so confidently in his arms. I'm getting used to the imprint his hand makes on my back and the way his fingers wrap into mine. I find myself wondering what the shape of his torso might be without his shirt. I shake the thought out of my head like a bad vision—him? Me? What a joke. He must weigh only slightly more than my Akita. It's the kind of item you read at the supermarket in the *Weekly World News* tabloid:

SINGLE, AGING FEMALE SCREWS HER LATIN
DANCE TEACHER.
(Cliché. Not that catchy.)
REDHEAD CRUSHES TOM THUMB MAMBO MASTER
IN TORRID TRYST.
All right, enough of this.

Besides, the student-teacher dynamic would never be breached. (Would it?) For him the dance floor is sacred space, and there are strict rules for what is appropriate and what is not while within its sanctum. *You must make eye contact; you must not step heel first; you must keep a slight bend in your knees; you must keep your back straight; you must maintain pressure in your fingers; you must align the crook of your arm with your partner's to sustain a correct frame.* He's full of these rules. He knows that this dance in particular, with its hip motions and gyrations, conveys an inherent sensuality. You can't lose your self-consciousness enough to learn it if you're concerned that the instructor has anything but the purest of motives. I mean, he has to project the trust-worthiness of a priest for a woman to really let herself relax.

(Granted, that priest metaphor is not the most reassuring, historically speaking.)

(But, really, this *is* only a dance.)

(And it's not like there's a test or anything.)

(And we *are* adults.)

(Nobody would know.)

(And it would heal any lingering "ouch" over Rafael.)

(*Un clavo saco otro clavo,* "one nail takes out another," the Spanish expression goes.)

(I've never done it with a short guy before.)

ENOUGH ENOUGH ENOUGH.

I become aware that he's proposing something to me. Says what I have to do is see how salsa is truly danced so that I can have an image of something to work toward.

Have I ever seen it? No, well, yes, in a couple movies—that doesn't count? The experience has never been captured on film? Bring a few friends and meet at a club? A field trip, as it were. *¿Por qué no?* Thursday is fine, day after tomorrow. The Conga Room on Wilshire, near La Brea. Sure, I can find it.

(Why is it that you never get any warning when your life is about to change radically? There should be big signs with bold lettering, like on the freeway, telling you what's ahead.)

As I'm walking toward the studio door, he calls after me. "Can I ask you something personal?" His voice, somewhat tentative. Asking isn't his specialty; he normally just directs.

I turn, put my hands on my hips. "Shoot."

"Do you ever wear dresses?"

What kind of a question is that? "Almost never," I reply.

"Why not?"

"Because I about had my leg ripped off at one point is why not," I say a little more defensively than I mean to. "I have a big, awful scar. Besides, dresses aren't my thing. I feel like I'm in drag."

He's giving me a TV-watching look, like he's waiting for the commercial to finish so he can see what happens next in the program. Then he saunters closer, boldly eyeing me head to toe.

"You need to forget about that scar. The only person who thinks it's ugly is you." He speaks softly. "You have a perfect shape. You would look beautiful in a dress."

I want to say that I stun him with a witty retort, turn on my heel, and stride confidently through the door à la Katharine Hepburn. What really happens is that I blush and look downward, mumble, "You think?"

He nods. "Really."

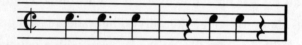

Nope. I'm not putting on a dress. Not even if I owned one. But that begs the eternal, unanswerable question, the koan of every woman's life: what to wear. I have an image of what might be appropriate cobbled largely from *Dirty Dancing* and Bacardi rum commercials involving plunging necklines and very tight pants. An exhaustive inventory of my closet yields workout clothes measured by the pound, a dozen pairs of jeans, countless riding breeches, three pairs of identical black slacks, one beaded evening gown I wore for reporting on the Academy Awards (two years in a row, but who ever notices or cares what freelance print journalists wear? We're the lowest end of the celebrity journalism food chain), one tailored black suit I have worn for covering the Golden Globes and for every semiformal media event of the past decade, and one leopard-print gold lamé gown in a size 14 featuring thigh-high side slits, a gift from Mom, who reasoned that since it went over big when she wore it to the Saint Francis Hospital Christmas party in 1978, it would work well for the aforementioned Academy Awards assignment.

I keep it in my closet in case anyone asks me to describe my mother. "Show, don't tell," the axiom familiar to all writers.

Shoes prove the most difficult issue: four pairs of riding boots, a few sandals, flip-flops for yoga, one pair of black heels I can't walk in for more than a block, and five types of sneakers. I end up at a local department store, taking most of an afternoon to ferret through the endless styles before uncovering a pair of Easy Spirit T-straps with a low, square heel, the kind of shoe great-grandmothers in Iowa wear to dances at the VFW. But I'm not proud, not yet at least, my main concern still being the ability to move without breaking another leg.

The only girlfriend game enough to join me on this field trip is Rachel, blond knockout Rachel of the full lips and endless leg, the type of pal who flies to Bangkok just because. Many I asked seemed intrigued initially but then withered at the prospect of a nighttime foray east of the 405 and south of Melrose, the interstate and the street that divide the tony Westside from the sprawl of the rest of Los Angeles. I wanted to rib them for being stuck-up, 'fraidy-cat little white Westies hopped up on wheatgrass and acupuncture, but realize that I can't throw stones, that whatever cool factor I might have once claimed is as finished as my twenties, that it's been nearly a decade since I ventured into a club or traveled much beyond the Westside myself.

So it's just the two of us, Rachel and I, standing on the sidewalk outside the club, our faces lit by the yellow neon of the Conga Room sign illuminated above. Around us people huddle in groups like schoolchildren, sexy brown women with rounded flesh bursting from gem-colored spandex and polyester, arms perfumed and slick with moisturizer; Asian women with bodies thin and pliable as stalks of new bamboo; women with skin like wet Concord grapes in jeans worn tight as a body glove. Then there are the men with coal-colored hair combed straight back and smelling of neroli, of bay rum; men with heads shaved, oiled skulls gleaming in the light; slouching men with the gold crucifix from their Catholic confirmation on a chain; smiling men with shiny shoes and pants with pleats; blond men who seem even paler under neon; men in the loose cotton shirts favored by Cubans called *guayaberas*, sporting posture so straight their shoulders create a plumb line.

My red peasant blouse with a keyhole neckline and my good old black slacks seem dowdy to me now. Rachel has opted for the short-flouncy-skirt look with heels so high she stands a good head above me. In fact she's so tall I half worry she might inadvertently tread on the instructor, who stands in front of us shepherding the way up a set of stairs covered in carpet that must have been new ten years ago.

"You weren't exaggerating," Rachel whispers close to me, her eyes on the instructor's small frame. Whatever my reply might have been is lost in the wave of sound that hits us, layer upon layer of percussion punctuated by the shriek of brass and the gravelly voices of singers, chanting words like an incantation to dance, *baile baile baile*. Immediately to the left is the entrance to a large room; high ceiling, dark wood floors waxed to a gleam, I'm thinking the room's the same size and shape as the sanctuary of Our Lady of Saint Albino, a church I love in Mesilla, New Mexico. Wrought-iron rails gird a raised platform where tables are arranged so spectators can watch the dancers below, but how could it be possible to just sit and watch when there's this music, like amyl nitrate shot straight to the brain. Fingers, feet— really every part of the human body is compelled to jump or tap or wiggle to these vibrations. It's the drums, the pound, rattle, and snap of a dozen kinds of percussion in concert. It's as if a spell is cast by your very own blood as it beats through your body.

I grip Rachel's hand, and she mine. "My god," we shout in unison over the music to each other. The word *teeming* was created to describe this space. In the glow of gelled lights coloring the dance floor, a rainbow of people whip around and against each other. A moving collage of arms raising, hips swinging, shoulders shaking, feet prancing. Flesh of illimitable hues, sizes of every proportion, press together. Fat people dancing with thin, old with young, short with tall. In motion, they are beautiful. More than beautiful, they are *alive*.

Rachel is immediately pulled to the floor by a man as tall and as blond as she, who will turn out to be from Israel and will want her phone number but won't get it because he's only twenty-three. I soon feel an arm around my waist. The instructor is at my side, a bend of his index finger telling me to lean my ear closer.

"Wanna see a short guy dance with a fat chick?" he says. (He really does say exactly this.) He points to a heavyset woman in a black shift standing rather awkwardly at one corner of the velvet rope that frames the dance floor. Her short, sandy hair fluffs out like soapsuds around her face, her pink frosted lipstick heartbreaking in its hopefulness. "This lady's a great dancer. Her balance is terrific. Watch."

He cuts seamlessly across the floor, appearing as at home here as he must be in his own house. I watch while he proffers his hand, a pleasant smile curling his lips, and I remember again that first impression over the phone, the courtly manner, the implication of old-world elegance. She returns the smile and grabs his hand, and as he leads her out toward the center of the floor he extends his arm, as if presenting the newly crowned Miss America.

As a new song begins he puts his hand on her back just below her shoulder blade to form the closed dance position, the two of them soon moving forward and back, as if stirred by a breeze. Then, a sort of alchemy as he begins to spin her around him, his eyes set to hers, the smile still on his face. She blooms under his touch, her feet fluttering like the wings of small birds. And, presto, he is no longer short, she is no longer fat; together they form something completely lovely. In the middle of this nightclub I feel the sting of tears come to my eyes.

In fifteen years of living in Los Angeles, I have been to the Skybar and the Bar Marmont and the premieres and the cool punk gigs and had the plus-ones to the galas that are said to be fabulous but never are and have crashed Arianna Huffington's book party and made out with a movie star and have lived in a house with a view of Zuma Beach, and I have never, ever been the right amount of thin or young or interesting or successful or ambitious or connected or talented. For me, this city has been perpetually cordoned into an endless series of waiting rooms, manned by stone-eyed sentries who are always looking over your shoulder for somebody better. But in this room there seems to hang an acceptance for what we are, this human thing. It comes on me like a religious conversion, the instant of satori talked about in Zen, the line between what came before and all that is possible after, the moment I know I want to inhabit this Los Angeles forever.

After the song ends he returns the woman to her spot at the edge of the dance floor. Her skin glows under the lights; her pink lips form a bright, upturned crescent. When he's back at my side I tell him, "I'm in awe. I've never seen anything like that."

"Thank you, baby." Right here's where I lose my name, to be called only "baby" or "babe" or "babes" or "lamb chop" or sometimes "lugnut" from this point forward.

He wraps his fingers around my wrist. "Your turn," he says.

Suddenly I couldn't be more panicked than if I were pushed into oncoming traffic. I tell him I can't; I tell him there's no way; I tell him I'm afraid I'll make a fool of myself.

"I'll take care of you; you'll be fine," he says, his arms already holding me in position.

"What if I do it wrong?"

"You will, so forget it. Have fun." His voice rises over the music. "Just step back, OK, just like we do in the studio. Look at me, don't look at your feet. One—"

He steers me, and for a moment I feel like pushing back, like fighting to not fall off a plank, but then I let go, allowing myself to be channeled by his arms. It seems that we actually float for a moment.

Then one of those shooting pains cuts into my bad leg, as if I've been bushwhacked with a hot poker—maybe it's the unaccustomed heels, the standing in line waiting to enter the club, but then again this happens to me a lot for no particular reason (nerve damage is a tricky thing)—and I freeze.

"Easy, keep going," he is saying, a knot of concern rumpling his brow. "I've got you; you're fine." When he lifts his left hand and places the other on my hip, I remember this is the cue to turn, and I try, and somehow manage to do that and return to the next step without stumbling. Then he and I glide back and forth again in the basic step.

The comfort of his hand on my ribs, the pressure of his palm in mine, the soft repetition of one-two-three he repeats for me ease me through the motions. Here's the part where the magic fairy dust sprinkles and—voilà—awkward, tomboy-ish, shit-kicker me becomes the pretty princess that all us girls, regardless of our age, secretly hope we have within ourselves. His arms around me form a perfect frame, a plat-inum setting for the jewel I feel I am in this instant. I record this as a moment of evolution, feeling for a second what it is to truly dance, and it is worth each stab that accompanies each step.

Then I lose the beat.

Can't hear it at all.

I desperately try to do my one-two-three, and it only gets worse, and I feel myself crumble, crash to a stop; the fairy dust dissipates.

But then I become aware of the pressure of his arms and see him nodding at me. "You can do this," he says, and he is steering me back again, over and over, covering the steps I miss, not allowing me to fail.

Three minutes, the length of my first real dance.

I hear Rachel. "You did it!" she says from the bar, cheering like I've won a gold medal, which is sort of what it must feel like, elated and exhausted all at once. The stabs of pain within my leg are coming on so strong, blood drains from my face, or so I imagine. It must be clear that something is wrong because the instructor puts his hand on my back and says, "Are you OK?"

"My leg." I look into his face and am overwhelmed with a sense of gratitude; it seems to me an extreme act of generosity on his part, to share even a taste of this ambrosial feeling all real dancers must know. I want more of it, I want all of it; this thing has hit my system, and I'm already thinking of the next time I can get it. Nothing has made me crave so much more, so fast.

I hug him, leaning down only a bit; right now he doesn't seem so short. "I feel like Cinderella."

His hand feels warm on the small of my back, his lips brush my ear as he says, "I'm glad, baby. That was enough for now. You want to go? Get off your feet?"

He walks us out of the club to the valet, me leaning on his shoulder as we wait for Rachel's pickup truck. After he waves good-bye she says, "Hey, your dance teacher's not bad."

"He's cute," I agree.

"He's got it for you big-time. Major big-time."

"Him?" I roll my eyes as if pantomiming shock and horror. "Please! He's my teacher!"

"Like that matters."

"Problem one, he's five feet shorter than I am. Problem two, he's five feet shorter than I am!" (It's no doubt clear by now that I tend toward hyberbole, exaggeration, inflammatory statements.)

"So?" she persists.

"Gee, maybe I forgot to mention that he's five feet shorter than I am."

"Who cares? Did you notice the way he was looking at you?"

"He's young, and he's Cuban. He looks at the entire female species like that. It's a cultural thing."

"Not at me he doesn't." (This is inconceivable.)

"He was being nice to me. I'm his client."

"Ah, excuse me, I don't think so, Miss Self-deprecation." Rachel shakes her head. "But, that's all right. I'm all for supporting your delusions."

I stretch out my throbbing leg and lean back against the seat. The view out the windshield reveals the straight black slick of Wilshire Boulevard in front of us. Billboards in Korean and Spanish brighten the night; they make appeals for foreign banks, and Asian car brands, and radio stations I've never heard. Scuffed metal grates cross like rusted accordions over the windows of nameless, closed businesses.

"I just want to dance with him. I mean learn to dance really well." I'm trying to feel that sensation again by imagining it, but it's like trying to recall details of a dream, dissipating the longer I concentrate.

She makes a right down La Brea, heading back to the freeway. "My guess is he'll be more than willing to help you out with that."

Rachel, she's such a cynic sometimes.

¡Merengue Workshop!

Get good at this easy, fast-paced dance. 1–4 p.m.

Appearance by Rudy "the Booty" Lorca!

Sign-ups through Saturday.

Dancing only gets harder.

My instructor is moving back to New York in June to work with some well-known Caribbean dance company, so suddenly there's the added pressure of a deadline: I have it in my head that by the time he leaves I must understand this dance, I must move together with another person with the kind of fluidity I have seen others possess, and somehow I'm convinced only he can endow me with this ability. Don't ask me how I came to this thinking. It's a common experience for students to become attached to their teachers, but this is really the beginning of what will become my fannish devotion to great dancers, who I suspect are actually manitous—supernatural forces masquerading as humans that hold the power to transform mortal existence.

The money I received for a big feature article did not go into a savings fund as planned, but to a package deal on biweekly private lessons. This is a secret I tell only Rachel and my other good friend J. (who once took tango lessons and understands how the desire to dance can come upon you like a fever). I've even spent eighty-five dollars on a pair of special dance sneakers (which, at the time, I think is a lot, not having any idea real dance shoes run about two hundred dollars a pair) and actually purchased stretchy dance clothes from a designer (Lisa Nunziella, a friendly contact I've consulted for magazine articles, gave me wholesale, but, you know, still . . .).

The investment hasn't delivered.

The more I want to master the dance, the more elusive the rhythm is, the more frustrated I become, the more I want to bawl and walk out. I am not sure why I don't.

It's already the end of April, for crying out loud.

"You're stepping on four. Why are you stepping on FOUR? What was the first thing you ever did? *Learned not to step on four.*" He breaks away from our dance to stop the music, his heels hitting the sprung wooden floor with uncharacteristic heaviness.

What these lessons have taught me so far:

- I have no native rhythm.
- I have no sense of timing.

- I have a rotten connection to my partner, which is measured by both tension and suppleness of pressure in the arms and fingers. I am either too slack, as engaging as a noodle, or too bullish, forcing my partner farther and farther away from me the longer the dance continues.
- I cannot be led. I'm like a puppy on a leash— I either jerk forward, or lag back, or dart sideways, anything but heel. It's as if my body revolts at the concept of having a man direct—even suggest—where I move, as if by allowing myself to be led I am personally driving a stake through Gloria Steinem's heart.

"Let's just forget this," I say as I too turn away, go to gather my things on the bench. "I'll pay you for this lesson and quit, because I'm paying stupid money to not learn this."

"Don't even talk like that," he is saying as the song begins once again. "Get over here, and this time you're gonna do it right. No mistakes. You're gonna see, and you're gonna get it. I feel it. You are going to do this."

He's wrong. I screw up immediately. Tears threaten on the rim of my lashes.

He drops his hands away from me and gives me an even look.

"You want the truth? Face it. You aren't going to get this today. You won't get this tomorrow or even next week.

How many lessons have you had? Seven? And you've never danced before? That means since February you've danced a total of seven hours. I dance seven hours in one day, and I've done that for ten years. Do the math." He leans back against the mirror, seems unperturbed. "This is hard. You have to practice."

My own arrogance knocks me in the face. I've been expecting to accomplish in seven lessons what he has perfected over a lifetime, as if dance were an easy thing, as if no art exists here, no suffering, no discipline, no magic.

"I'm sorry," I say as I come back into position, our elbows touching, hands clasped, my fingers cupping his shoulder. "I reckon you're right."

He snickers a little. "Did you just say 'reckon'? *Reckon?*" He mocks my stress and tone.

"Listen, there are a few things you have to know," I say, suddenly spoiling for a fight. "My uncle was a rancher, I was raised in rural New Mexico, I lived in a goddamn trailer, and sometimes, yes, I do say words like *reckon.*"

"So? Who told you any of that matters?" He presses his hand tight around my rib cage. "I accept you for who you are. Always." I avoid looking down into his eyes by turning my head to the side.

"Babe, you don't got to be like that with me. You're far from me now. Don't be far." A strand of hair has wound its way to the corner of my eye, and he reaches to smooth it from my face, tucking it behind my ear. "Let's try it again. No big whoop."

So, I can't help it, I sleep with him.

He had invited me to see him perform. The invitation sounded innocent enough but was a calculation, I realize now, because he knows that onstage he is the essence of balance, a weightless ribbon of movement. And sexy? Oh, sexy. The crowd stood in ovation, and I quickly left as soon as he exited the stage, my face burning, embarrassed at the realization that for the past two months I have been asking the veritable Gene Kelly of salsa to drill one-two-three, five-six-seven, with me, and I still can't keep time to save my soul.

The next week, an offer to meet him at the Mayan, a downtown club known as the temple of L.A.'s Latin nightlife. At the end of our lesson he'd seemed fidgety, as if he were waiting for something.

"What?" I finally ask, unable to stand the suspense.

"I was wondering, have you got anything going on tomorrow night?" He talks quickly, and it occurs to me, surprise surprise, he's actually nervous. "I mean, you're probably busy, which is cool—"

(In couples dancing, there's something called "back leading," where the follower anticipates the move the leader is about to make. This is a horrible, fatal fault in a follower, because you can easily misread the lead and end up ruining the balance of the dance. It's also disrespectful, a form of telling the leader you don't believe he's doing a good job. However, like most bad habits, it's easy to fall into—especially if you've been around long enough to know the basic patterns. And, sometimes, the first few moves with a new partner can be tense, as you're anticipating what might happen and you want control of the outcome. Personally, I can't tolerate tension of any sort and I hate feeling like I'm not in control, so I back lead all the time.)

"I'm going dancing tomorrow night," I tell him.

"Really? Wow. Good for you. Where're you going?" He's nodding as if making casual conversation, but I see his shoulders slump.

"I'm not sure—where am I meeting you?" I have a wide, tooth-and-gum smile that I've been told can look attractive in a Farrah Fawcett kind of way if I tilt my head at a certain angle. That's the smile he's getting right now.

I give myself forty-five minutes to get to the club, about twenty more minutes than I really need, but it's downtown, and I always get lost in L.A.'s downtown, which I privately suspect is merely an extended backlot of generic cityscape created by Disney, the streets being a tangle of one-way routes and no-right-turn intersections. I still get lost going to the Los Angeles central library in daylight, so no telling where I could end up at eleven o'clock at night trying to locate a club.

On Hill Street I find a line half a block long, the thump of music audible from the street, young bodies pressed together as a tense herd. So this is the infamous Mayan. I am thinking about Chitzen-Itza, the ruins where the Maya used virgins for blood sacrifice and played an ancient form of soccer using the heads of conquered enemies. They were a fierce people, the Maya, their culture marked by the interlacing of sex, death, and spirituality.

When I left the house this night I worried that in trying to look sexy I'd instead only managed a certain "vampire chic"—pants with enough spandex to shrink-wrap my ass, ruched short-sleeved top with a deep V neckline and push-up bra–enhanced cleavage; the black of it all making the white of my skin appear nearly albino, and the red of my hair all the more vivid.

He meets me on the street, and the first words out of his mouth are *dios mío*. Now I'm thinking it was the right call.

I take his arm because taking his hand would look awkward, and we pass through the velvet ropes, a surprising number reaching out to greet him: *Qué tal, buenas noches, oye, how's it going, man, I saw you in that magazine*. I have to confess excellence turns me on. I admit, it's my version of star-fucking: a person who has achieved excellence at something—dancer, mechanic, stockbroker, poet, cook, surgeon, plumber, butcher, baker, candlestick maker—always has my attention.

The Mayan is a dark, multileveled labyrinth of red carpeting and faux stone, a dank assault of cigarette smoke, booze, cologne, and sweat. I feel a predator's intensity radiating from the frank stare of each man as we move toward the dance floor, and it seems there is actual fire in their eyes, and to tell the truth I am heated by the burn of them, by the uncommon experience of being appraised purely on the basis of sexual appeal. (Let me just say it has a rightful place on the scale of human experience. Too much, a problem; none at all, another problem.)

On the floor, a compelling, undulating fervor is created from so many bodies whirling around under the blinking white-and-black of strobe lights. I can't relax and so am as useless as a stick; here's Mr. Hot Shot Salsa on a public dance floor with a beginning student. The pressure's too much for me. Going one on one with Shaq, doing crossword puzzles with Noam Chomsky—some things simply should not be attempted.

Because of the crowded swirl of wet skins, we can't move in the classic salsa pattern, so we are smashed against each other. It hits me then: all I need to remember is that he's a man and I'm a woman. I know *this* dance. I turn my back to him and let my body find its rhythm against him, a churning, ancient feeling, and all at once the beat is coming from the floor into my feet, spreading through my legs, trunk, arms—like water traveling from the roots to the branches of a tree.

I lean forward and feel his hand press at the base of my tailbone, another on my thigh. Our hips lock and move together. When I turn back around, his face has turned the color of merlot. I think he might pass out, but he grabs my hand and yells over the music, "Let's go upstairs."

Couples huddle in the dim light at the top level of the Mayan, which forms an amphitheater over the main dance floor. We sit next to each other with a primness that belies the dance we just shared, and it seems neither one of us knows what to say next. Then the music changes into a frantic, marching beat punctuated by the brassy shrill of horns.

"What kind of music is this?" I yell.

"Merengue," he says, leaning so close to me that I feel the pop of his breath on my ear as he speaks. "I hate this shit." He tells me merengue originates from the Dominican Republic, that no one really knows how it started. Some say that a hero in one of the island revolutions was badly injured and so danced with a kind of dragging step. Out of respect to his sacrifice, people imitated the movement. Others say the dance came from the slaves in the plantation fields marching in their chains to the relentless beat of a drum.

"Which do you think it was?" I ask, but he motions like he can't hear my question, so I move my face closer to his as he inches toward me. In that collision our lips brush for a second, and I see that the bottom lashes of his eyes are as long and curly as the top, framing his eyes in a deceptive softness. Then he spreads a hand over the nape of my neck. "We're getting the fuck out of here now," he says.

In the parking lot, he kisses me and tells me I was the most beautiful woman at the Mayan that night, and it made him proud to be with me. It is, I've since heard, exactly what he says to every other woman before she gives him head in the front seat of her car, but in that moment I feel, perhaps, it could be true.

In salsa, as in any other style of formal dance, somebody has to lead, and somebody has to follow. Who does what has been, for centuries, based on gender. Man initiates, woman responds: he tells you how far to spin away, how fast, when to come back. The sexual politics dancing externalizes might appear crude and antiquated in the wake of the seventies sexual revolution, but in fact the dynamic is much more subtle. A good leader has to read the abilities of his partner, and a good follower has to demonstrate what she is capable of and comfortable with. When the relationship between partners is symbiotic, they can craft a perfect dance.

Sometimes I still think about how it was between him and me the first time. It comes upon me at the strangest moments; I'll be in traffic stopped at a light and suddenly the images will jump to the forefront of my mind, and I'll be seized by a warm, swampy feeling in the hammock between my hips, and pretty soon the car behind me will honk, and I'll realize I was deep into the memory of that night.

I see him walking toward me on the pocked downtown sidewalk under the streetlights' tungsten glow, fog in the air making the picture grainy, diffused. He steps as if in shoes light with helium or some other element that defies the concrete world around us. He's looking sideways, like something across the street has caught his attention, but there is nothing but darkness, so I think maybe he's trying to avoid the moment when he looks at me. He's like that. Doesn't ever want to appear anxious.

Then I see him in the front seat of my car, his white shirt unbuttoned, his pants unzipped. I did that. For some reason, it surprises me that he has hair on his chest, a black trail leading down between his legs. I hear us breathe, deep gulps as if we have just come up for air. One of his hands has slipped past the firm padding of my bra and now gently kneads the pulpy flesh underneath. This is a backstreet that has no name, really just an alley between warehouses where he parked to avoid the charge for valet. Yet it's only a block from the Mayan, so in theory, although it's almost one in the morning on a starless L.A. night, there could be people walking by who would observe us. Maybe some have. We wouldn't have noticed, and it doesn't matter. This is like those times in Paris, like that crazy time in Ciudad Juárez, like a time in Sydney, like another time in a backwoods

Vermont motel. Not my part of town, therefore off the record.

I say, What now?

Immediately he replies, We're going to your place.

It's far. The Westside.

We're going to your place, he repeats. I'm following you. Let's go.

He zips his pants and gets out of the car without kissing me. Instead he puts a hand between my legs, cups the curve of Venus mound with his hand, says something in Spanish I can't understand. His Cuban accent is different from the Mexican Spanish my ear is tuned for, his words quicker, cut off at the ends, the *s* swallowed.

What am I thinking on the twenty-minute drive to my house? Strangely, I feel resigned, as if this has already been written somewhere. I admit I am bothered by the logistics of having sex with a man so much physically smaller than myself. In my thoughts I appeared huge, like the female praying mantis over the tiny male of that species. Those bugs are believed to kill their mate after sex, and I am prone to a certain ferocity; I could imagine taking his throat between my teeth and biting down hard.

I have done this before, taken a man to my house, but I can't remember feeling so nasty about it. That's the word, *nasty*, like I am crossing into a lawless no-man's-land. What happens next: As he parks his car I shut all the blinds and light a candle. The orange flame provides the only light in the room. I sit on the bed, and he stands next to it, his hands framing my face gently, his kisses lighter than I expected, the push of his tongue shallow and hesitant in my mouth. There's the taste and smell of salt about him, a sort of brine, a savory flavor that I will forever now associate with serious dancers. His hair curls in ringlets around my fingers but has a fine texture. Black, though already turning gray at the temples. My hands run up his chest, down the smooth length of his back, this boy-man, the sallow cast of his skin warmed by the candle.

Maybe I say, How do you want it?

All at once he's rough, jerking my hips around until I am on my knees on the bed. I feel feather kisses on my spine but his hands harsh and bruising at my hips, how quickly he buries himself inside me. The mixture of soft and tough a narcotic to me—God, I am so wet, I think for a moment there might be some kind of hemorrhage—and then there is a staccato beat, not at all like the lightness of his dancing, a one-two-one-two beat. He prefers to dance salsa, but he fucks merengue, the slave dance, the low dance, the salamander movement and machine-gun fire merengue is all about. Funny that he hates merengue, calls it a pointless dance, but perhaps what he means is that he thinks it is base, too primal to be social, too crude and without the necessary nuance that for him makes dance a sacrament.

I think of a hummingbird, all quickness and light and surprising strength. He makes me feel not like a big, awkward white woman but like some kind of gardenia that such a bird would naturally go into. His hands wind through my hair as if he is pulling my head to save me from drowning, I don't know what he is saying; for whatever reason I taste rum on my tongue, green olives, sand—where is the sand?

Final picture: the waves of his hair press against the Egyptian cotton pillowcase. He's turned away from me. His shoulders are no wider than a girl's, but his arms are toned and rounded with muscle, the downy hair of his arms the color of tar, a black that in candlelight reflects nothing.

Suddenly he raises his arm, says, "Get over here, baby."

It is a relief to me that he talks like this. At least I've met a man who knows what he wants.

I scoot to curl myself against him, my breasts pressed against his back, my arm around him. Naked against each other, my skin is colder than his, as if some kind of marble, the most tanned places on me still paler than any spot on his body.

He lays his hand over mine. Baby, he says, go to sleep.

We wake up at the same time to the blaze of late morning slicing through the blinds, or maybe what stirs us is the clink of my dog's tags against his collar. I look to the other side of the bed and realize his eyes are open. He says, You have a beautiful smile.

I feel myself brace. Now is the moment of the requisite

bullshit, the time when a man feels obligated to say meaning-less, insincere, stupid things he does not believe but imag-ines he should say. I'm expecting poetry; I'm expecting him to tell me, I can change your religion, be the face of God for you if you want to see it.

But instead he says, *¿Sabes que quiero?* I want to fuck you, then I want you to make me a sandwich.

Advancing in the levels:

Before proceeding to Salsa II, you must know the progressive and side basic, and how to turn to the left and right in salsa timing.

I think of a picture I have of Mom, age five. The pale pink of her pointe shoes looks white in the photo, her tutu pure as snowflake. For some reason there are homemade antennae attached to her head, shining with what I think is tinfoil; perhaps she is meant to be some sort of dancing butterfly. Her red hair was once said to be the color of new pennies, and curly. Now it has fallen out. Or rather, a bald spot grew so large that even she could not deny it. She's shorn her head and now wears a bright red wig. Her hair is starting to grow back, though, but it's rough and straight, pasted to her skull, which, to my surprise, is

relatively small. I always think of her as large, the kind of
force that creates her own gravitational pull, but she is so
far from that now I wonder if that idea has always been the
exaggeration of a child.

I've come to visit for the weekend, and we sit on the porch
of her doublewide this late afternoon to watch storm clouds
boil over the serrated shale peaks of the Organs Moun-
tains outside Las Cruces, New Mexico. She gets up from
her lawn chair to swat at the spastic pug she calls a dog, and
loses her balance for the hundredth time today, tottering
and weaving like a small dinghy cast out on an angry sea. I
notice a bruise bluing the side of her left temple and figure
she must have fallen earlier today when I heard a noise in
the bathroom.

"Well, hello there," she says, plopping back down in
the chair. "That was pretty swift."

"Nice save," I say, wanting to encourage her rather
than getting mad at her again. I am sick of hearing the
chronic judgment in my own voice over what she has and
has not done and feeling that the time for annoyance is far
gone. I am trying to ignore the tremble of her hand. I tell
her about seeing salsa at the Conga Room and how it's
inspired me to keep taking dancing lessons.

"From the dwarf?"

Despite all my best intentions, somehow she always
gets to me. "He's just short, it's not a condition. For chrissakes, Mom."

She has this way of lifting one eyebrow. "Have you slept with him already?"

Mothers do know their daughters. I take a quick sip of coffee, a strong brew we drink at her house from morning until early afternoon, when she switches to Scotch. "So?"

"Samantha, you can't sleep with a short man. It brings a curse on the woman's family," she says matter-of-factly. "That's what the witches say."

Let's consider just a few random facts: she lives in a trailer, my only permanent mailing address is a P.O. box, we've both gone bankrupt at various times, I have a metal leg, her husband died, mine divorced me for good reasons, my father left her pregnant, my grandfather ran out on my grandmother when Mom was a child, our uncle blew his own head off with a shotgun, and she's been playing the same lottery numbers for the past decade but still hasn't won a red cent.

"Maybe in our case it'll have the reverse effect," I tell her. "We can always hope."

She ignores me, instead says she's glad I'm trying to dance after all this time, that when I was a little kid she gave me the choice between ballet and riding lessons. "I said, 'Sammy, do you want to be a ballerina or a cowgirl?' and you went for the horse over the tutu," she says.

"Why couldn't I be both?"

"We didn't have the money," she says, "and you thought ballerinas looked like sissies."

Mom herself did both, riding and taking dance lessons three days a week for most of her childhood. She quit riding after a bad fall at age twelve but kept up the dance lessons until she was eighteen, when she joined the air force. My grandmother loved horses but she certainly didn't dance, so dance lessons had to have been Grandpa's idea.

"Sure," Mom says. "Your granddad was a helluva dancer. But you know that."

"How would I know that?" I ask her. I knew him only after I got to college; when I was a child he refused to see me because I was born illegitimate, or so the story always went when his ex-wife, my grandmother, was telling it.

"You mean you never danced with your grandfather?"

"Nope." I don't remind her he died six days before my wedding, or that Gram had a fatal stroke a month before that day, which would have been the only time I'd have had the occasion to see either one of them on a dance floor.

"Too bad." She takes another drag off her cigarette. She's switched to the light brands that come in pastel cartons, my only clue that she has, somewhere, acknowledged the deterioration of her health. "I took ballet forever, and that was everybody's idea. It's why I'm so graceful now."

"Yeah, it's really carried over."

She laughs at herself. This is a good sign. "At least I have nice, strong legs."

"So, Mom, you could do all those old dances? The fox-trot and the waltz?"

"And the Charleston," she says. "But, you know, I could never get down that low, because my muscles catch."

She rests her hands on her stomach and looks across the street of her mobile home park, as if she is surveying open range, as if she alone can still see the jackrabbit and the beetles, the turtles and scorpions, the dry creosote bush and prickly pear that rightly should still cover this land. The furrows deepen between her brows, two auburn-penciled arches against the pallor of her skin.

It is said through any path that leads to mastery, there are three stepping stones: Great doubt. Great faith. Great persistence.

I'm all about doubt, doubt that I can ever get this dance or any other for that matter, doubt that I even know what it is I'm trying to get. The uplifting sense I felt in my first lesson and the euphoria I experienced at the Conga Room are dim memories at this point.

The studio is empty this late afternoon save for one other instructor and his student, an older Korean woman in a bright red dress and matching shoes. Unlike in salsa, which has the partners boldly lock each other's gaze, their faces turn in opposite directions, and they hold each other in a porcelain embrace, circling in the gentle wavelike motion that is the Viennese waltz. There is no music, only the shuffle of their suede-soled dance shoes across the far corner of the waxed floor. I wonder what they are thinking about. Maybe she is imagining being held in the arms of a man she once loved, or maybe she is merely counting steps. I would like to think he is appreciating the beauty of this woman no matter her age, but maybe he's only calculating how many more years he will do this before he too can retire, or why the studio just jacked up its rates for floor time.

In this, my first lesson since the Mayan and my visit to New Mexico, respectively, I find a comfortable familiarity has filled the spaces where sexual tension used to linger. But that's not to say he's become forgiving and supportive; if anything, he's more demanding than before.

I make the mistake of trying a side step as he makes a turn, and I manage to screw up the rhythm, quickly getting off count, beyond even what he can cover. He stops, shakes his head.

"Women start sleeping with me, and they start thinking they can dance," he says.

"I know what you mean. Men start sleeping with me, and they start thinking they can read."

"Funny." He takes my hand, starts the rhythm again. "Leave the jokes to me."

Then he snaps his fingers and points to a spot on the floor about two feet from him. This is his shorthand; what it means is, at the end of the turn you're making you should end up right there, and if you end up anywhere else, you've failed.

I extend my left leg, take a deep breath, and twirl twirl twirl like a wobbly red top across clean linoleum.

"Well that was"—he puffs out his cheeks and exhales loudly—"absolutely awful. *¿Qué coño es esto, mujer?*"

The translation for that is, "What the fuck is that, woman?" *Coño* ("cunt" but often used like "fuck") is one of those Spanish words—like *pendejo* ("idiot"), *pinga* and *verga* ("cock"), *mierda* ("shit"), *chingón* ("fuck"), *cabrón* (asshole), *maricón* ("fag"), and *puta* ("slut")—that I know well, having grown up as a *güerita* or *gringa* ("white girl") in the small towns of northern New Mexico, where most everyone is what they call there Hispanic, or sometimes Chicano, but never *Latino,* which is a word I only heard used once I got to California. In any event, given that the educational process is pretty much one protracted *Lord of the Flies* experiment, developing fluency in the worst possible words is useful for surviving and even flourishing within junior highs and high schools, where the vast majority of students are raised bilingual. Of course, this gutter vocabulary does me no good when I'm at a restaurant, or watching *Despierta America* on Univision during breakfast in the kitchen with Nacha, or with the guys who work with the horses at the stable, or giving a group of students from Uruguay directions on campus, or listening to the salsa recordings I have begun to put in my CD player—in other words, pretty much any quotidian situation I now find myself in. It does, however, equip me with the ability to understand the particulars my dance instructor is trying to convey regarding my lack of progress as a student.

"What?" I say, frustrated. "What more should I be doing? I'm counting the steps like you said—"

"Chill, OK? Calm down." He takes my hands. "The thing is, you're not letting the dance unfold. You're trying to rush it. You're trying to control it. You're not getting that you don't have to do anything but just be there and dance. Instead you're trying to help, but it's no help, and you're not letting me lead you."

He pauses for a moment. "Let's do this. Pretend you're me; I'll pretend I'm you. Now try to turn me."

I do. He's unmoving, a brick of granite. "That's what it feels like leading you."

Ironically, I consider myself very easygoing, accommodating even; to experience myself as someone who is difficult to move gives me pause, and I wonder when and how this extends beyond the dance floor. So I try again, but this time all the strength suddenly goes out of my bad leg, like someone turned off the power switch, and I lose my balance, which was not great to begin with. I fall flat on my butt.

I expect him to laugh, but instead he seems more impatient. He pulls me up by the arm. "Come on and do it again," he says.

"My leg—" I begin in protest.

"That whole thing about your leg, realize that's just an excuse." He's telling me this like he's talking about the weather. "The reason I became such a good lead is that I had to learn ways to compensate because I'm short. Everybody's got something. That's what makes us the dancers we are, OK? I'm short, and you've got a metal leg. No big deal."

We pick up the beat, and here comes my turn. I hear the pop of the congas in the music, and I think of a leaf floating on top of a babbling brook, and I imagine feeling light like that. His arms buoy me.

"Now *that's* what I'm taking about!" He smiles broadly but then grabs my hips, presses his thumb to the pelvic bone. "Hey, you've lost weight." An accusation. "Where's your ass, baby? You've got to start eating more. Pasta, pasta, pasta."

He's telling *me* this. Me, who has spent all of my life after age eleven trying to lose weight. Me, who once had a (white) man say he thought he could love me if I lost fifteen pounds.

Oye, viva Cuba.

We take a break, my reward for making the turn. He's leaning his back against the window at the studio, his legs spread wide as he sits on the bench, his jaw slightly slack, and I imagine he is thinking about patterns and turns, fine-tuning whatever routine he is creating at the moment. Maybe he's thinking of his dance partners, or his girlfriends, which, I'll hear later, are sometimes one and the same and sometimes not. I'll learn what they all have in common are plump behinds like pork roasts, and hamlike thighs. He loves the fat on women.

He nudges me with his knee. "You know how it is when you've been eating just shit food, hamburgers and shit, and you're still hungry all the time?"

I nod. He leans forward toward me, his eyes trained on my face.

"So you're hungry all the time; then you have a really good meal, like Thanksgiving, and you feel totally satisfied. That's how I feel after having sex with you." His voice is not seductive; in fact I've never heard him ooze anything that might remotely be construed as smooth talk. He's just gabbing, as he would about sports. "I mean, I don't even want to fuck anybody else right now."

It has to be understood here that a lot of men have told me a lot of things over the course of my life, but no one has ever likened me to turkey and mashed potatoes.

"That's such an original compliment," I say. "Maybe you could write greeting cards for a living if this dancing thing doesn't work out."

He slaps his hands together and guffaws. "I'm just like Romeo, man oh man. *¿Qué culo, no?*"

It occurs to me that I'm sleeping with a man who laughs with his mouth wide-open, for whom sex is as elemental and uncomplicated as eating. He is a person of appetite, in all measures. I stand up and extend my hand to him. "Juliet is ready to dance."

Strangely, salsa starts to infiltrate my life long before I make any measurable improvement on the dance floor. The first to notice is a priest at the Zen Center where I often attend *zazen,* the morning meditation. In between the sitting periods there is a silent walking meditation known as *kinhin,* in which the goal is to have complete awareness—the feel of your bare feet across the wood floor, the experience of your breath as you inhale and exhale, yadda yadda yadda. In my head, the pop of the conga and the tack-tack of the claves start playing so loudly I honestly consider that it might disturb my fellow meditators in their evident serenity. Worse, so vividly do I start to replay my dance teacher's lesson in how to place my foot to achieve the rolling movement called Cuban motion, I unconsciously begin this toe-heel, toe-heel step as I walk in line during the meditation.

I become aware that one of the black-robed priests is at my side. "Mambo *kinhin?*" he inquires softly, his eyes sparkling. "Very nice." (That's what I like about Buddhists; they usually have a good sense of humor.)

And then I'm riding Harley. It's just a regular Saturday ride under a hot sun, until the sound of his hooves over the sandy earth begins to take on a distinct tempo. Suddenly my ear is picking up the rattle of the dirt hitting against his iron-clad hooves with every trot, sounding something like

the dry grating of the wooden *güiro,* a percussion instru-
ment often heard in salsa. *Quick-quick-slow,* I'm thinking,
quick-quick-slow, as I rise and fall in the posting rhythm, up
and down in the saddle. Such an easy flow between us, my
horse and I, earned over ten years together through some
of the best and worst times of my life. Then, for the first
time, I truly understand that in these years what he has really
been is my dance partner, the two of us creating a beauty in
form and motion under saddle that we could not accomplish separately. My job has been to be the leader, to harness
and show off the loveliness and power that is this 17-hand
Thoroughbred, with a coat rich as chocolate. Because now
I know what it is to be led by an expert leader, it makes me
sad to realize I have not always been so, too tough in the
turns sometimes, not clear enough on the direction at other
times, starting us off on the wrong beat more often than
not. But Harley is a generous soul and has always forgiven,
always been willing to come back with me to the arena that
is our ballroom.

It's as if a box full of snapshots falls from a shelf in my
mind, scattering images here and there. I see scenes from
the day of our accident: Harley and me on the trail; I'm getting off to cross the small stream; my urging him to cross,
my impatience; him rearing back in fear; the flash of his
dark legs and the shine of metal hoof as he jumps and lands
on top of me. The red of my own blood, too much of it to
be believed. This is so clear to me now: What if I had been

a better lead? What if I had not pushed him in spite of his evident fear?

As I slow him to a walk I'm overcome by a sense of love so strong I lean over in the saddle and throw my arms around his big neck. Then I hear what sounds like applause.

"Bravo!" Edward and Kate, the stable owners who have been close friends ever since Edward literally saved my life the day of my accident, stand at the side of the arena. "You guys looked great out there," Kate calls.

Ten years, and this is the first time anybody has ever spontaneously broken into applause upon watching us complete a dressage pattern in the arena. Harley stretches out his neck and shakes his head, his ears flopping.

I wave back to them. "Hear that?" I ask Harley.

Salsa II

This series focuses on cross-body lead, spot turns, stop and go, the pretzel, and strengthening your leading and following skills. It is recommended that you stay in Salsa II for at least 3 months.

And so it came to pass that my instructor left for New York.

"Who am I going to take lessons with now?" I say on this, his last morning at my place, as he's trying to get my dog's hair off his black pants and asking me if I'll "loan" him a white T-shirt so he can look halfway decent for the private lesson he's got in a half hour because, *mira*, this shirt is wrinkled beyond salvation and it looks like the dog slept on it, *coño*.

I hand him a cotton T-shirt. "Well, this was fun," I say in a kind of last-day-at-summer-camp tone. "I wish you the best in New York."

"Why are you talking like good-bye? Like we're never going to see each other again?" he begins, looking down at his wrist as he fastens his watch.

It honestly never occurred to me that we would; I'd already billed this event to my girlfriends as "the 'little' fling with my dance teacher." I tell him that there are three thousand miles between Los Angeles and New York; I tell him I've got things going on; I tell him that I'm not one of these women who confuses sex with having an actual relationship. Much. All right, a few times I have, but not often, and certainly not now for double damn sure.

"Of course we're not going to have a *re-lay-shon-ship*, that would be stupid, but I'll be back here, you go to New York. It's cool." He kisses my neck. "It's all good."

The romantic might hope this is merely bravado on our parts, that there is real love or something like it happening here that we are just not acknowledging. In fact, there is not. There will be no Richard Gere waiting outside on the fire escape with roses in his teeth, no Richard Gere in a navy officer's uniform come to sweep me off my feet in the middle of the factory. (Every romantic vision in my mind has to do with Richard Gere.) The feeling between us is different. I don't have a name for it. It is, perhaps, acceptance.

"So, really, whom should I take more lessons from?"

"Let me see . . ." He ticks off a list of names, with commentary—so-and-so is a little too "ballroom" (by that he means stiff), so-and-so is geographically desirable but not very good, so-and-so will give me bad habits, so-and-so doesn't do well with beginners—until finally he says, "I love Laura, she's the best, but you might want a man—"

"No!" I say. Perfect! A dance instructor I *won't* sleep with. One is an experience; two and three means a pattern. "How do I get ahold of her?"

✔ **I still have the notebook where I jotted her informa-tion on the cover: Laura Canellias, "Salsa Diva Produc-tions."**

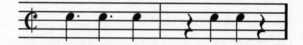

Every once in a while, some friend—always a married, suc-cessful one—gets the idea to fix me up on a blind date. The intent is always well-meaning, because I know my friends worry about me. Sam Dunn, among the throngs of other professional, heterosexual women in their late thirties with-out a mate, the voracious majority of the singles population, biological clock the size of Big Ben, covering the dating landscape like locusts. Oh yes, my friends do worry about my future, so they set me up with what I call "candidates," that is, single men who have great jobs, good education, are older than I am, and want to settle down. These men tend not to have a prison record, current restraining orders against them, membership in any group ending with the word *Anonymous,* or wives and/or girlfriends they "forget" to mention. In other words, men who in no way would be attracted to me, or I to them. A brief history:

- The psychiatrist from the university medical center. If he told me again how in touch he was with "a woman's needs" and how at home he feels with his own feminine side, I would have suspected him of actually being a tampon.
- The guy who drove a black BMW, worked as a vice president at an envelope-making business, and talked about his ex-wife. For three entire hours.
- And how could I forget the navy JAG lawyer who broke into a profuse sweat upon our meeting and spent a good portion of the evening in the restroom, but otherwise seemed very nice.

This time Lauren calls to ask me if I'd be interested in meeting one of her former coworkers. "I've been thinking so much about you and that horse guy and then that dance guy, *oy vey*. Darling, I'm telling you, you need to see a better caliber of individual." It's worth noting that while Lauren is not Jewish, she uses a lot of Yiddish in her speech, having been raised the only Chinese kid in an otherwise Jewish neighborhood in Illinois. It's also worthwhile noting that Lauren is a working actor, so if she wants me to meet a coworker, what she's actually doing is trying to set me up with that most ubiquitous of L.A. bachelor: the Actor. Which, no offense, but come on, "better caliber"?

She intuits my reaction, perhaps from the silence coming from my end of the phone. "He's not one of *those*," she assures. "He works! Did you see *Desperado*? He was a bad guy. *Fools Rush In*? He was the ex-boyfriend. Remember the Hispanic paramedic on *ER*? That was him."

Did *I* see *Desperado*? Please, only about six times, but at that point I really only noticed Antonio Banderas. (This was before Melanie.) I even made my friend Janet go see it for full price in a theater, a fact she has yet to let me forget. "Can't place him, sorry," I admit.

Like any good yenta, she lists the indicators for our successful potential match, having to do with compatible careers and education level, et cetera, et cetera—the stuff that usually sounds the death knell for chemistry—but then adds, "And he knows how to Latin dance. He was even a dancer for a while on Broadway."

I'm not joking; even my dog, lying at my feet on the rug, pricks up his ears at that bit of data. Of course I acquiesce, and then we talk scheduling. He's going to be on location filming something for a while, then I'm going to be in New York working, so it looks like the mystery date can't happen for at least a month or even two. I tell her to give him my number anyway, what the heck. I'm about to hang up before I realize we've neglected one vital piece of information. "Lauren," I ask, "what's this guy's name anyway?"

"Carlos Gomez."

This is more or less how it happens: I enlist my friend J. to go on a fact-finding mission to the new studio my dance teacher told me about, a place in West Hollywood located above a dry cleaners and a bakery, respectively. Let's say J. is one of my closest friends, which is true, and let's say for the hell of it that she makes independent films—the no-ending, simmering-pathos variety that French people make, although she's not French, but could be, being a Juliette Binoche beauty with a Michel Foucault intellect who always looks lovely even while being—how do I say—a little odd. She's the kind of person who will explain the relationship between quantum mechanics and mental health but gets lost on a five-minute drive to the Ralph's supermarket in her own neighborhood.

This studio, with salmon-colored walls and framed paintings of couples in tango, conveys a dramatic serious-ness, opposite the chintzy quality radiated by the street-side place on the Westside where I've been going. While dance is one of the most elevated artistic expressions humans can undertake, dance rehearsal spaces tend to exude a tired, workaday quality, even when they are well main-tained, as if the fatigue that results from bodies working so hard actually becomes implanted in the physical space. But I digress.

When we tell the man at the desk we're here for the salsa class, he quickly looks us up and down with an appraiser's eye. "Beginning? Studio C at the end of the hall."

J. and I marvel at how he intuited our skill level; on our way down the hall we invent a history for him, say he's a Gypsy from Romania cursed by "the sight." Now we know all he had to do was look at our shoes: her heels, bought especially for a few tango lessons, hardly even broken in; my Easy Spirit T-straps, evidence that I had yet to invest in serious footwear and therefore had not made a real commitment to The Dance.

The studio is the size of a volleyball court, framed by mirrors on one end and arching windows on another. We're among the last to enter; more than two dozen people already face the giant mirrors and are doing the basic one-two-three step, forming rows in a sort of ragtag chorus line.

Were I asked to draw a sociologic profile of the typical salsa student from this bunch, I could not. The U.S. Census says that Los Angeles is the most ethnically diverse city in the nation, but only in this dance world do I find the tangible evidence of it; for the most part L.A. functions as a loose configuration of unofficial nation-states based on race and income. This group is fairly evenly divided between men and women, though ranging widely in age: some baby boomers, some twenty-whatevers, some clearly retirement age, some—thanks to the wonders of modern dermatology—impossible to tell. A woman with hair braided in long cornrows has brought her teenage son, whose face is set in concentration as he tries to follow the steps. Men in business suits look to have come straight from the office; there are women in dresses and heels who might work at a bank, others who might run the bank; others wear jeans and T-shirts; a groovy few look like they stepped out of a yoga class; one brave soul sports baggy shorts, white socks, and dress shoes.

Working in the media and residing in places like Malibu and Hollywood's tattered fringe have exposed me, if often only from afar, to some of the most famous, glamorous people now living on the planet. These people are not those people. I feel relief because I'm not one of those people either. But am I one of these people? There's an on-the-sidelines quality to how I experience my life; perhaps it is an occupational hazard for those who work in journalism—present but always one level removed, always reporting, the stakes never really personal.

But what I meant to tell you is that there, praise be, in the center of humankind itself, stands she, Laura Canellias, Salsa Diva, Queen of the L.A. Scene.

"All right, everybody, be honest, how many of you are singing 'wonton tomato' along to this song?" the diva intones over the music. "Try *Guantanamera*."

The divine form of the Holy Mother is commonly seen in Latin cultures, where Catholicism has for centuries been planted in soil that once nurtured rich indigenous belief systems. The American Southwest is no exception, the sublime easily coexisting alongside the prosaic. Where I grew up, people are totally comfortable with the idea that the form of the Virgin Mary herself can appear within an enchilada, or on the side of the barn, or that her statue on a shelf at the Wal-Mart can begin to cry real tears. Our Lady reveals herself in everyday areas as a beacon of hope for all, to enlighten our impoverished spirits and to remind us to seek our better selves, as God would have us do, hallelujah.

Laura is performing in a hokey little show for a party after this class, but J. and I don't know that; we think she always appears thus, in a chartreuse bodysuit with bell-bottoms and bat sleeves, lined in puce with the hems beaded in coordinating colors. Her long, wavy hair is the color of molasses, and her preternaturally youthful figure—the signature of every professional dancer—is a configuration of gliding curves, like brushstrokes on a canvas, creating an image Diego Rivera might have painted, a common elegance born of sweat and faith, flavored with just a touch of sorrow. What must be gold glitter twinkles from her hair. Her talk is pure Texan, San *Antone* as they say, wide and flat and plain. Her heels appear to be made from purple snakeskin; her nail polish is gold, hands and toes matching. Although we are not close enough to actually smell her perfume, the essence of tiger lilies and jasmine surrounds her.

She is, in a word, *magnificent*.

"Ladies, don't let me see your hands flop down over your wrist like that when you dance," she is saying over her headset microphone. "It looks like you're begging, and, honey, let me tell you, ladies don't ever, ever beg."

We are in the year 2003, which means Laura has been teaching salsa for twenty years, being one of the very first teachers of this particular art in Los Angeles. Any of the literally thousands of people she has taught over two decades will agree she is patient to a saintly degree, that she intuits exactly what you need to learn and knows how to teach it to you. This is partly the product of a lifetime of formal dance experience, from jazz to ballroom, teacher training at Arthur Murray, countless nights performing in clubs around the world, and working with movie choreographers. The other part of it is the rich kind of compassion some people develop after they have struggled and sometimes achieved and sometimes been brokenhearted, after they have wanted and worked and dreamed, after they have been hurt but started over anyway.

Even before I know any of this, it's evident to me that Laura's not a *diva* in the much-used sense of the word, nor is she a queen per se. No, it seems obvious that Canellias is actually the present-day, Tex-Mex incarnation of Qwan Yin, the Buddhist goddess of mercy and feminine virtues. Another possibility is, yes, la Virgen de Guadalupe, revealing herself as Carmen Miranda.

"Everybody, grab a partner and make a big circle. Gentlemen, you'll be rotating, so let's have you on the inside." She waves people into place, then steps into the clearing of the circle. She snaps her fingers and beams a kittenish smile. "In my classes, the men come to the women; we don't go to you. As it ought to be in life."

I'm not embarrassed to say I adore my yoga teacher, an ethereal fairy of a woman, a Sikh convert named Gurmukh, who taught me how to pray and showed me the path to respecting my body after the accident that damaged my leg. Something about Laura makes me think of Gurmukh. I would not recognize the profundity behind the Salsa Diva schtick if I hadn't first known Gurmukh, although to look at the two women, it would seem they are literally night and day. Gurmukh the morning star, Laura the full moon.

"This is the person who's going to teach me to be a dancer," I whisper to J. as we stand with our partners, waiting for instruction.

"Oh, oh, me too!" J. nearly jumps up and down. "I don't want to learn from her, I want to *be* her, on a cellular level, inhabiting that dimension . . ."

See what I mean? A little odd. "Right," I agree.

For the record, it's impossible to become a great dancer by taking only group lessons. If somebody already knows how to dance, fine. Or if they're among those prodigies with a kinesthetic genius that allows them to pick up any physical skill by osmosis, fine. (I try not to hate those people.) But for the simple majority of us, group classes really provide a laboratory in which to practice not only the steps of a dance but the endangered skill of interacting socially with complete strangers. It becomes achingly clear to me that we have forgotten how to touch one another, we who touch more molded plastic than we do human skin on any given day.

Lew stands in front of me, a balding, happy-smile man whose button-up cotton shirt is already drenched from the exertion of the warm-up, and, possibly, the nervousness that must come from walking up to women you don't know and taking them in your arms. We're instructed to form the "open dance position," meaning we're basically just facing one another, holding hands. I feel a deep tremor coming through his fingers, his hands not shaking so much as vibrating in the bones.

I introduce myself, smile, and try to make conversation. "So Lew, what do you do?"

He returns the smile. "I'm an engineer at Lockheed."

"Did you dance much before this?"

Lew shakes his head.

"Really? So what made you want to take salsa?" It occurs to me that I don't know how to make actual conversation. I know how to interview people, which is different, and is not a comforting process in the least. I realize this because Lew's face just became awash in what appears to be terror.

"I, well, I just thought it would be fun."

The music begins, and Laura sets off the count, "ONE-two-three." Lew misses the beat, but, alas, I forge ahead, creating a collision between us. "I'm sorry," we say in unison, and he insists, "No, it's my fault, I'm supposed to start us off," and I kind of fall in love with Lew right then, want to hug him close and tell him it's fine, that the effort to try is all I really want, a feeling I will have repeatedly over the next hour with Joe and Pedro and Tony and Mohammed and Kung and Larry and Welton and the young boy whose name I don't catch because his voice is not much louder than a whisper. It seems to me this night that a corner of the world is saved a little by a simple dance class, because nobody looks good, because everybody is taking the chance to break free of this "quiet desperation" that has become white noise in the back of our lives and to risk embarrassment and failure, but perhaps to reach, at some point, if only for a moment, the heart's desire.

J and I had approached Laura Canellias after that class with the enthusiasm of groupies rushing the stage, begging to get on the tour bus with the band. "Why sure, I'd be happy to do that for you," she'd replied warmly after we laid out our proposal to jointly study with her, at least until the time we ceased to feel like baby elephants on a dance floor.

As we were leaving she handed us a flyer for a concert on Friday, a big-time band from Cuba called Los Van Van. "If you like salsa, you have to come. Y'all can sit at my table. All the *salseros* in town will be there," she said. We no doubt gave her blank looks, because she then provided definitions: *salsero,* man who dances salsa; *salsera,* woman who dances salsa. She did not explain the negative associations that can, depending on whom you talk to, often/ sometimes/always/never come with these labels:

- *Salsero* = man who develops severe allergy to committed relationships because his dancing ability allows him to hold mass quantities of women in his arms any night of the week.
- *Salsera* = woman who judges not only a man's attractiveness but his very worthiness to exist on the planet based solely on his ability to keep tempo and provide a great lead.

These I figure out soon enough.

J.'s husband turns out not to be enthusiastic about his wife attending a late-night salsa concert without him; nor will he attend with her, as he would rather face an IRS audit than dance. That's how I find myself on this foggy June night in the company of Shannon and Lori, a beloved former student of mine and her friend, crazy-girl types up for anything that involves alcohol. They are also from the Valley, so there's no need to talk them into driving "over the hill," as if it's a trek requiring a passport. This freedom from Valley phobia is important, because that's where Sportsman's

Lodge is located, the kind of place rented to families for wedding receptions or to the Elk's Club for fund-raisers. Sportsman's isn't normally considered a hoppin' venue, but, then, I've never seen it occupied by what appears to be all 38,664 of the Cubans said to live in the county.

Imagine a salsa prom, everyone revealing their interpretation of what it means to be dressed up: I smell the stout aroma of cigars, smoke wafting in from the parking lot, and the suggestion of tobacco on men's hands. The high-pitched murmur of women's voices flows around me, a pouring of Spanish words from which I can catch only one or two. Standing in line at the lobby entrance, rhythms boom from inside the walls, my pulse jumping at the syncopation of the drums, the way the beats arrive just ahead of my expectation, a roller coaster of sound. Then entering the grand ballroom, an area large enough to accommodate two dance floors. Light from the chandeliers makes clean hair shine like crow feathers in the sun. I look for Laura among the white-linen-covered tables as the crowd weaves through to the dance floors.

This night at Sportsman's is probably the one where I see her up by the stage in low-slung red pants cut with a long slit up the leg, spinning and bending like salsa's own Salome around her partner, a young man in a wheelchair, who is leading her with one hand as he moves his chair in tempo to the music with the other. So this is a *salsera;* a woman who exudes sensuality alongside elegant femininity and makes any man feel that he's her prince, at least for the three minutes a song lasts. I'm suddenly laden again with my familiar awkwardness, a chronic condition since childhood, and can no more imagine myself looking like that than I can imagine solving a physics equation.

Think of dancing like swimming: Private lessons are the wading pool. Group classes are the community YMCA swimming pool. Dancing socially is to jump into the middle of the Pacific Ocean and take your chances. Come to think of it, maybe it's more like studying a foreign language in school. Take Spanish, for example. You soon find out when you get to Madrid—or Miami for that matter—that studying in the classroom and getting good grades on the homework bear no immediate relationship to your ability to go shopping or catch a cab. You know basic words and the grammatical theory of how the language is structured, but you're missing a lot of vocabulary and don't have the ear to decipher all the possible variations in pronunciation, the infinite and unique ways people choose to express themselves. Should you suddenly need to survive in this new environment, given only your schoolbook skills, you will be, in a word, *screwed*.

Shannon, Lori, and I find Laura's table. The point is moot, however, as we don't get to sit down at it for at least an hour because we're instantly besieged by offers to dance. Perhaps it's that we radiate the intangible pheromone that tells men we can't dance but would like to, so are obviously not discriminating. I warn each man who invites me to dance that I'm a beginner, which, this night at least, seems to elicit a protective reflex from my partners. The sweet older gentleman with the silver hair and gold-capped teeth doesn't seem to mind that I manage to plant the heel of my T-straps over the instep of his foot not once but three times. The lanky man with blue eyes and skin freckled more deeply than my own keeps the count for me with Swiss precision, despite the fact that my feet seem to want to do their own thing anyway. "Sorry," I say fifteen different ways, in whatever language I can think of, *"perdóname,"* "apologies," "oops," "forgive me," "didn't mean that," *"discúlpame,"* "excuse me," and finally, "well, shit."

Then there is the man from Panama. Here is the character who confirms the unfortunate usefulness of stereotypes, in this case, the lounge lizard: polyester shirt of Studio 54 vintage, which seems to have actually been made without the first four buttons; numerous gold chains worn with no sense of irony; a thin mustache meant to recall the dashing impression of Zorro; and beautiful, thick, wavy hair sadly managed by Jheri Curl, grown far past his shirt's oversized collar. I dance probably six songs with this guy, one tune blending into the next. I lose my balance on every turn, causing me to be thrown against his chest. As a consequence he turns me about every fifteen seconds, jerking my

arms this way and that, and I imagine what a daddy long-
legs spider must feel as its gams are plucked out by a curi-
ous boy. I hang on because every once in a while I manage
to find the beat and get to practice my steps for a count or
two before being whirled off again.

Sweat is soon stinging my eyes, my impressions of the
room taken as if by time-lapse photography. Nubile dancing women who wiggle like fish on a hook and men holding
instruments crowd the large stage. Around me, flashes of
billowing skirts, squares of wood parquet, black pants, cotton shirts, the ivory of teeth. Yet my eyes keep being drawn
to the end of the dance floor, to a corner table where a man
sits all alone.

I do experience this exact phenomenon: the earth stops
revolving for a full second, and I see this man so clearly it
is as if I am standing right in front of him. His large, dark
eyes seem wise and a little sad, ropy veins move over
the muscles of his hands, his black suit is fitted to a strong
physique, the fine weave of his shirt like white orchi—

OK, skip the poetry. The guy is just fucking hot. Hot-
Latin-macho-dude kind of hot. You get the picture.

I'm thinking, *Why can't I ever meet a guy like that?* A man
who is sexy, mature, confident, obviously appreciates this
music, and likes to dance. Implied in this, of course, is that
he is also the man who makes me laugh (on purpose), who
enjoys the smell of horses and likes it if the dog sleeps with
us, who reads the *New York Times* in bed on weekends
regardless of the city in which he lives, who wonders at things,

who shares secrets, who can handle my mother and gets along with his own, who misses me when I'm gone because there is no one in the world he would rather be with, who makes my breath catch in my throat a little every time I see him, who is the voice I am always glad to hear, who knows I love flowers even though I never ask for them, who makes me feel more of myself rather than less of myself when I'm with him, who would like a kid to call him Dad. And he has his own scars, and he teaches me the feeling of having found home.

The earth, as it must, starts to revolve again, and I am still crashing into the Panamanian lounge lizard. When the song finally ends I thank the man but insist I need to rest, and so he—as does any man who respects the protocol of formal dance—leads me back to my seat at Laura's table. On the way I scan the room for another glimpse of the handsome man, but he has been swallowed by the crowd.

Laura herself is at the table, her long nails painted tonight a bright maraschino. This I notice because she holds an elaborately patterned Spanish fan, waving it with quick strokes toward her face in a genteel effort to dry perspiration. Other women sit at this large table; they are, I will learn, a sort of coven of dancers over age thirty-five who hold Laura as the high priestess of salsa. They too flash their fans, and many other *salseras* at the surrounding tables do likewise, like the sudden descent of monarch butterflies in spring.

I only wonder at it then, but I will come to know what *salseras* say behind those fans. They talk about dancing. All night. Who is a dream lead; who dances on the second beat, or "on two" the old-school mambo way; who can't find "the one," meaning the first beat, to save his pathetic soul; who pulls you off balance in the turn; who is a famous dancer but it's all about him, so that you are nothing more than an ornament; who holds you too tight and gives you the creeps: who won't dance with whom and why; who might get good with a little more practice.

Of course, much more meaning is embedded between the lines, because when it comes down to it, all we're ever really doing is talking about men and about ourselves. Of the men, it's of the ones who didn't call back, or the ones who forgot the rent money, or the ones we are either in love with or thinking about breaking up with, or the ones who are sleeping with *her* but *she* doesn't know it, the ones who are our fathers, the ones who are brothers or the sons we worry about, the ones who are dead so we went to a *santero* in Pacoima to throw *los cocoas* for answers from the spirit world and it turns out everything is fine. We talk about this to one another because there is no more soothing balm in the world than female conversation, because no matter who comes and goes, another woman is there to listen, and in this way we talk our way through life.

Laura asks me what I do, and I tell her I'm a writer, that I am indeed writing an article about salsa, which is an abbreviation of the circumstance, because what I mean is that I'm going to have to think of something to write for some publication real quick so I can justify all the money I'm spending taking lessons. My editors at the magazine are becoming increasingly annoyed by the fact that I seem to be able to do nothing but present ideas that are all about salsa, which they have said they're not interested in because it's too "marginal," and by that I think they mean "ethnic." They remind me that my contract is soon up, and they rely on me to "spot trends," meaning figure out what Jennifer Aniston is eating for breakfast, to which the response rumbles upward from the core of my being: WHO GIVES A FLYING FUCK?

Anyway, where was I?

The band takes a break between sets, and the DJ comes on. I ask Laura if we can sit down sometime so I can pick her brain about why she thinks people are drawn to salsa, and she says now's as good a time as any, being that she's pooped out from dancing all day, and I consider the Panamanian and I say, yeah, I'm done dancing for tonight too, so I pull out the little notepad I always keep in my purse and we lean in toward each other to talk over the music.

"It's all about connection," she says, her long silver earrings swaying with the movement of her head. "A lot of times people think they're just coming for the exercise. So many times over the years people have come to me and said, 'I want to learn to dance because I have a desk job and don't use my body,' but they discover something else."

I don't tell her I was coming for sex, but the exercise is what I found. Sure, sex too, but what I haven't mentioned yet is that weight keeps melting off me, so much so that the other day I bent in front of a full-length mirror to adjust my socks, and for the first time in my life as a healthy adult I could clearly make out the knots of my spine as my back bowed. The only time I was thinner was in a hospital bed on a morphine drip, but I must say, as much as I liked the morphine, this is more fun.

Instead I just ask, "So what's the something else?"

"It ends up balancing them in so many ways. They learn coordination and grace, and they achieve partnership with another person." Laura's eyes are so dark brown they appear to be all pupil, fathomless, never revealing all the heartaches that have led this most skilled of *salseras* to be solo in life even as she provides so many with the tools to join together. But that is not rightfully my story to tell.

I realize how deeply I yearn for precisely what she promises salsa will deliver: coordination, grace, partnership. I think again of life on my little iceberg, and of the great blueness around me, and of all the pursuits I have engaged in—yoga, Zen, writing—that have given me a complete self, but no human I want to share this self with. Only with Harley do I feel complete. Given that he's a horse, that probably sounds a little strange.

Laura is talking: "Dancing has rules. Where else can you act out your sensuality in a safe way with another person? God knows I've had some dances where it clicks, and, girl, I'm telling you . . ." She leaves the details to my imagination, seeming to be caught for a moment in the memory of those dances. "After the seventies free love and AIDS and all the other things that have come along, nobody knows what the hell to do. We have to learn to relate to one another all over again. For us women, we need to learn to be feminine again, and that there is nothing to apologize about in being feminine. Men have to learn how to take charge, but without jerking us around. Ideally, what we learn in the dance is to empower one another."

Truth? Laura doesn't say all this at once the way I've just written it, although she does say most of it exactly like this because I have it in my notebook. Some of it she said in one of the three weekly classes I take with her; some over margaritas and guacamole at El Torito; some while I pilfer through the Imelda Marcos–sized collection of dance shoes housed in but one of her four closets; and some said on the night I got dressed at her house for a costume party, arriving straight from the barn, dust covering my boots, a green mark that could only be horse shit on my pants, hair pulled tight underneath my lucky Adidas baseball cap. I'd forgotten both my change of clothes and my makeup bag, but within an hour I was showered and transformed into a French can-can girl, complete with fringed velvet dress and a satin choker, such is the vast repertoire of Laura's wardrobe. That was the night in late September—or was it October?—that she taught me how to apply false eyelashes, a skill involving glue and Q-tips my mother always said I needed to learn but which I ignored. That night, Laura also initiated me into the sorority of women who know the joy of fishnet stockings. Not only do they act like a girdle on your legs, vanishing cellulite, but they effectively cover scars, even bad ones. In the morning you wake up with diamond patterns cut into your skin. A small price.

I forget how the night of Los Van Van ends. I think Shannon and Lori go home before I do. I seem to remember one more dance, with a man who doesn't speak any English, but I am too shy to practice my Spanish much, or maybe I think it would be impolite to make him suffer both my dancing and the mutilation of his native language.

I scan the room for that handsome man, but I don't see him again. The table where he sat is vacant.

Beginning New York on 2

This six-week series introduces dancers to the Palladium style of breaking on the second beat. Timing and turns will be drilled. Intermediate and above only. See front desk for details.

Horse people are weird. I state this freely, being one of them. We are the kind of people who feel most comfortable in the company of creatures not of our own species, and we frequently suffer huge gaps in socialization skills. This is why I can never understand the logic of having "barn parties," those social events where humans are expected to interact at the place they normally go to escape one another.

Which brings me to what I'll call the Fourth of July Barn Party. I say yes to attending because Kate and Edward made a point of telling me they hoped to see me there, and I don't want to disappoint them, and besides I'm leaving tomorrow to work in New York for a few weeks and want to make sure everything's in order for Harley while I'm gone. Of course, the minute I arrive I'm already plotting when I can politely leave, what with everyone standing around clutching their plastic cups of wine, talking about the West Nile virus and vaccine updates, thumbs hooked into the pockets of Wrangler jeans. The jangle of old Rolling Stones tunes comes over a stereo speaker piped from the tack room as Edward busily arranges a stage and microphone near the arena so that his daughter, Thaïs, can soon entertain with her acoustic guitar.

I mosey up the incline to the area where Harley is stabled, where rows of covered paddocks are separated by a breezeway down the center. I see the line of heads as the horses hear me approaching, the expectant faces hopeful that I have extra carrots to dole out. When I whistle Harley whinnies back, which I always take to mean, "Oh good, you're here, what'd you bring me?" His stall is the last on the end, and when I get there his head is arched far out, ready to rifle my pockets for the peppermint candy he knows I have hidden.

I'm scratching Harley's ears as he eats the candy when I hear the strains of what I think is a rumba coming from below. Edward. He knows about my recent fascination with tropical rhythms and so has put on a Latin jazz recording. I begin a little dance there in the breezeway, moving my hips and shoulders.

"*¿A ti te encanta esta música*, Miss Sam?"

It's Daniel, the foreman for the ranch, asking me if I like this music. He stands in the breezeway with a wheelbarrow loaded with alfalfa bales. I call him Maestro because he was a schoolteacher in Mexico, and he will often help me with my Spanish homework and has begun speaking to me only in Spanish, though he is far more fluent in my language than I am in his. I often wonder if economics alone led this bookish man away from his classroom in southern Mexico to work as a ranch hand here, or if there were other reasons. He could be teaching children how to read but is instead taking care of horses for equine hobbyists in Malibu. *Qué lástima,* as the saying goes.

"*Si, Maestro, me gusta mucho.*" I do a few little steps, and I tell him I'm learning how to dance salsa, in case the demonstration wasn't clear. "*Yo estoy aprendiendo a bailar salsa.*"

He lets out a small chuckle. "*Bravo, pero esta canción no es salsa. Esto es són. Es diferente.*" He sets down the handle of the wheelbarrow and tells me he lived in Cuba for many years; in fact, that's where his children live with his ex-girlfriend. This is news.

"I thought the beat sounded different," I tell him in English, wanting to pry into the details of why he left Cuba, if he misses his children, but for once think it is perhaps better to wonder. "Can you show me how to do the *són?*"

He looks around the stable. "*¿Aquí?*"

"Sure," I say, putting my hands out as if in the closed dance position around an imaginary partner, and then I ask him if he wants to dance. "*¿Quiere usted bailar con mi?*"

"*Con migo,*" he corrects me. "*Chica loca,*" he says, laughing, but comes to put his hand, rough and square, at my back, the brims of our dusty baseball caps nearly brushing. *"Suavecito,"* he instructs, move softly. He steps back, and I inch forward following the best I can, in the reverse of how I have been taught. We begin a slow shuffle in a sort of zig-zag step, different from the back-and-forth motion of salsa I know from my lessons, but yet the feeling is somehow familiar. Our workboots kick up small clouds of sawdust and dirt in the breezeway on this warm day. Daniel and I smile at each other, the silence between us filled with the music from the reedy speakers below and the quiet rustle of horses.

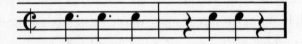

Three messages on my voice mail: the first from my mother, reporting a vital bit of news about how one of her dogs has begun to bark at the Australian crocodile hunter on Animal Planet; one from J., who is going to New York with me and has found us cheap rooms at the midtown Holiday Inn; and another from my dance instructor.

"Hey. So are you coming out here or what? Let me know." Click.

Warms the heart, doesn't it?

I take comfort from established methods of doing things, I like the fact that I can learn these methods, and I like that these methods have served to give millions the same experience. For example, when a man takes me in the closed dance position, he puts his hand not on my waist but at the end of my rib cage. It is more respectful of personal space but, most important, allows him to easily direct my weight forward, back, or side to side. I lie the length of my arm on his, cupping the front part of his deltoid muscle with my palm, a position that looks delicate but also creates a subtle brace for balance. These points are not random; they're the underpinnings of the frame that allows the dance to occur. Yet to watch a couple in motion, the eye can't detect the subtle biomechanics that support the dance, any more than the eye can delineate the engineering that allows the Brooklyn Bridge to hang so beautifully over the East River.

Of course I'm only imagining the bridge and the East River, because for eighty bucks a night in midtown all you're going to get is a view of an alley and a brick wall. J. reports a similar vista from her room across the hall, but it's not like we're picky. Besides, this is merely a one-night pit stop before we take the train upstate to a writing program. We're getting ready to meet my dance instructor, a five-minute cab ride uptown; he's doing a demonstration tonight for students at the new studio where he's teaching, after which the three of us are supposed to go out for drinks.

I think it must be J.'s idea for me to wear a dress, as I can't imagine it's mine. I rendezvous with her in the hall for our outing. In her white summer dress, she looks like someone out of a Lancôme commercial. I'm wearing the same tired thing I wore to the Conga Room: red peasant blouse and the T-straps. She says (as she has said many times), "Oh, pal, no . . . let's go back to my room. I've got something I want you to try on."

That J. says this makes even more sense when you know that in addition to being a stunning, weirdly brilliant film gal, she used to design clothes. Her highly developed sense of aesthetics is coupled with that rare husband who supports her refined shopping tastes. And, by the grace of my salsa weight loss, she and I now wear the same dress size, or, rather, I can now fit into a size 4 that's a little too big on her, provided there's enough spandex in the material.

Only through this unique convergence of factors do I end up in a dark blue sheath dress that fits my body like new skin, the square neckline and narrow straps revealing far more of my breasts than any bathing suit I have ever worn, the hem hitting just at the knee, at the top of the first of my scars.

"Va-voom, Versace, va-voom!" says J., assessing me from every angle, as if dressing her Barbie doll. "Donatella sure does know what looks good on an Italian girl."

Italian girl. No one has ever put that label on me before. Technically speaking, I suppose, I am, as my father arrived in New York directly from Italy, then turned around and headed straight back there a few months later. Only three things have ever been said to me vis-à-vis my looks and my mysterious paternal legacy:

1. My grandfather: "Sammy, if you never tell anyone you're part dago, they'll never guess, because
your face doesn't show it."

2. My grandmother: "Those hips and that waist of
yours, they're sure not from *our* family."

3. My mother: "Why do you always wear black?
What are you, some sick Italian peasant in
mourning? Put on a little color, for godsake.
Here, try blue eyeshadow to match your eyes."

I go into the bathroom so I can examine the transfor-
mation under bright light and big mirrors. The person
in the mirror appears attractive in a womanly way, red
shoulder-length hair, glossy lips. It seems to me I haven't
met her before. Then I notice the large scar around her calf,
the other white gash at her knee, and I recall exactly who
she is.

"I can't go out on the street like this." I point to my leg.
"Look."

"You can hardly see that! You're the only person who
even notices!" J. protests. "You have to wear this dress,
have to, have to. Put more lotion on your legs while I go get
something."

I do what she says because she hasn't steered me wrong
yet. She quickly returns holding a pair of strappy sandals
with a sexy little heel. "Here," she says. "The neutral color
makes your legs look longer."

I don't pick my closest girlfriends based on us having the same shoe size; it just conveniently works out that way. I put the heels on, and she claps her hands in glee. "Oh, goodie!" she says. "He's going to have a heart attack."

He is waiting for us on a corner off Broadway, the blacktop of the street and the sidewalk made shiny from a late afternoon rain. He's dressed sharply in black pants with a ruler-straight crease, crisp white shirt, his belt and shoes polished to a gemlike luster. It's evident to me that this city is his natural habitat, so much does he meld with the monochrome colors and the angles and lines of the architecture.

He doesn't notice us emerge from the taxi across the street because he's talking animatedly on his cell phone. Not until we're about ten feet in front of him does he stop, as if suddenly caught in a tracking beam, like a character in a sci-fi movie. He really does end the conversation with whomever he's talking to on the phone by saying, "The weather's lousy, but the view just got a whole lot better. Later."

He greets J. with a quick hello and then just stands in front of me, his mouth parted loosely, his eyes on my face—and then every other part of me. No words, for once. His silence is one of the most sincere compliments I think I've ever received.

Finally he closes the distance between us and slides both his hands around my waist, spreading his fingers over my back, gripping me to him. I tilt my head down and kiss his temple; his lips graze my collar bone.

"Thank you so much, baby," he says softly.

I whisper this in his ear: "You're welcome."

In the morning we stand in the hallway at the Holiday Inn waiting for the elevator, a languid energy between us that a shower did not wash away. Reaching barely past my shoulder, he stands so arrogant, so confident. A question out of nowhere pops into my head: "What would you do if you weren't a dance instructor?"

"I'd be a male escort." His mouth twists in a wry smile.

"And the difference . . . ?"

"Be nice," he says as the doors to the elevator open, revealing an empty box.

"Did you ever want to do anything else?"

"Nothing," he replies. He puts a hand on my back, leading me into the elevator. "Everything in my life comes from dancing. Everything. Like you. Say you'd never seen me dance. I'd just come up to you in a bar. You going to talk to a schmuck like me? Am I going to get anywhere with a woman like you?"

I consider what he might mean. What is a woman like me? I have a wonderful career; I am at least five inches taller than he is; I am six years older; I am not Latina.

One of the few pictures I have of my mother and father suddenly pops into my head. In the photo they're looking into each other's eyes as if about to kiss, my mom's long auburn hair pulled into a chignon at the base of her neck, her lips rouged, my father's light brown hair cut neatly, a green sweater over his shoulders. I'd never been able to understand how they got together in the first place, since they literally did not speak the same language and, by her accounts, had nothing in common outside of the fact they both loved to dance. He was an engineer with a foreign company consulting on a Pennsylvania dam project, evidently an educated man from a bourgeois European family; she was a working-class Irish-American girl raised by a divorced mother in a time long before that was common. Now I understand: details that would likely prove to be barriers in the outside world become meaningless on the dance floor. And when you're dancing, it's easy to believe you'll always be dancing.

"Well? Would you?" he asks again, his expression flat.

A group of loud German tourists crowd in, and we move to the back. There is an odor of sunscreen lotion, a badge of optimism against this cloudy day.

We stand in silence.

"I didn't think so," he says finally, pushing the button for the mezzanine.

He looks up at me. The black frames of his glasses suddenly make his face seem smaller; the cruel greenish cast of fluorescent lighting reveals acne scars. And me, exposed in this light like Cinderella the morning after the ball. I feel like a dried-out, day-old pastry left too long on display. I picture the always harsh trenches around my mouth suddenly appearing deeper, furrows carved into my brow, stale remnants of last night's makeup ringing my eyes, and, somehow, I have the feeling that I missed the particular season in a woman's life when she can consider herself truly beautiful.

The Germans exit on the second floor. When the elevator doors close and we are left alone with the security camera, he urgently presses himself against me, a hand wrapping into my hair, pulling my head down to meet his lips, his tongue darting lightly into my mouth. We smell of the same harsh hotel soap we shared in the shower, and I also catch the scent of my hair gel, which he must have used to slick his curls into some semblance of order.

I feel a collapse of something inside, a deep sense of relenting, and I allow myself to acknowledge that, at this moment, I want him more than I have wanted anything in a very long time, so much so that my knees do in fact feel weak—this is not mere cliché. I reach to put my hand at his back and realize I can wrap one arm entirely around his body. An odd fit, him and me, not two anyone would put together from the packaging. The mismatch of our shapes makes for a peculiar sensation of androgyny. It's not unpleasant; more illicit.

Then the elevator bell dings, signaling our arrival at the mezzanine, and we pull apart. When the doors open we are standing as if two strangers. The truth is, we don't match. We never will. And we both know it.

J. and I spend three weeks in New York. I don't dance, but I do have the chance at a block party in Brooklyn the night before we leave. J. and I stumble in with a friend of a friend, who had understood from the cousin of her building's superintendent that a salsa club was opening on Union Street. It was like that old childhood game of telephone, or I think there might have been a problem with translation, because what we found at the address of the supposed salsa club was actually a get-together of Puerto Rican families celebrating a son's return from his tour of duty in Afghanistan.

We make profuse apologies for the misunderstanding when we show up at the door and quickly make to excuse ourselves, but shouts from inside insist no, who cares you're complete strangers, come in! We have plenty of food! *¡Por favor, comaselo!* Come, eat, have a beer, dance! *¡Toma cerveza y baila, baila!*

Caribbean beats boom through a portable stereo, tunes I've heard before in class. "Who plays this music?" I ask a man standing next to me in a tank top and flip-flops, looking like he just arrived from the beach.

He eyes me with undisguised disbelief, as if to say, even a *white* girl should know the answer. "This? You don't know Tito Puente? He's the godfather of salsa, you got to know Tito," he admonishes. "He's Puerto Rican! Hey, where you from, honey?"

Everyone in the room seems to be swaying with the beat, a gritty, more grinding movement than I've seen before. J. leans into me. "Notice how everybody here inhabits the rhythm."

Yes, inhabit, the perfect description. I have never felt more foreign; dance lessons can take you only so far.

Partygoers frequently stop to hug or kiss a young man next to us with his back against the wall, his dark hair buzzed in a crew cut, his posture ramrod stiff. Of course this must be the soldier returned home. He looks no older than twenty, his cheeks smooth and babyish, and it shocks me to realize that probably not more than a week ago he held a gun and felt sand grate against his skin. A different air seems to hang over him; he's in the crowd but not part of it.

He catches me staring at him. "Ma'am," he nods politely.

I'm caught for a moment between feelings of wanting to thank him for his service and despair that he had to go at all. Nothing seems appropriate to say. I think about asking him to dance, but I don't have the confidence. "Glad to be home?" I manage finally.

"Yes, ma'am," he says, but his expression is impossible to read.

I don't hear from my dance instructor for the rest of the time we're in New York, although I do leave him a message when we're back in the city. "Why am I so annoyed by that? It's super casual between us, and I really do want to keep it that way," I say to J. as we wait for our flight at JFK. "So, tell me, why am I bugged?"

It's early. She's trying to sleep behind her sunglasses in these most uncomfortable of plastic seats at the American Airlines gate. "Because you want to be the one who doesn't call," she says.

"Exactly! Further evidence you're a genius."

She pats my hand. "Just as well. Aren't you supposed to have a date with—what's his name, Chuey Gonzales?— Lauren's friend? Maybe he'll call when we get back home. That's something to look forward to."

"*Carlos Gomez,* Einstein," I say, batting her lightly on the head with the magazine I had been not-reading. "Anyway I'm the Chicago Cubs of love. I don't have much faith this one will be any better."

She puts an arm around me and rests her head on my shoulder. "Have faith in Carlos Gomez, sweetie. If not in him, then somebody."

Back in L.A., the newspaper tells of boy soldiers like the one I met in New York being blown apart by car bombs in a desert so far away. A heat wave in Europe this year is killing thousands in France, in Rome dogs are dying on the leash, but here in Southern California we exist in a tender balm of marine layers and breezes that ruffle leaves.

It is August. Each night now I fall asleep to the rattle and shake of old Cuban men singing island songs, a sound track given to me by a friend for my birthday. Everyone in my life now knows of my salsa habit, and so gifts of music have come, even from my ex-husband and his wife. They burn a Latin jazz CD for me, and he labels it by hand with a black Sharpie. "CubAN," it reads, a mix of upper- and lowercase the way he has always printed, since he was a teenager. I smile at the letters.

The claves and *tumbao* become the current that I float on into dreams, or maybe my skin really has turned cool and slick like the pelt of a snake, muscular too, winding through a jungle of green, through terra-cotta tiles and an oak-finished banister filigreed with rusting iron. On my tongue is the scent of roses and plumeria and the musky acid of a man's sweat against my animal breast. In my dream I am tireless, beyond the pain of an aching leg, spinning tightly as if suspended from invisible wires, not listening to music but inseparable from it, as from the pulse of my own blood pounding in my ears.

Then the jungle colors change; everything becomes bleached, a tangle of starched white hotel sheets. Over the beat comes the roar of Fifty-second Avenue below a tiny ninth-floor room. His dancing shoes are under the bed; the rhythmic clack of the headboard against the wall angers the guests in the next room. "Shut up in there!" they yell, but I do not hear them for the force of his breath in my ear.

You should be with me, he repeats, over and again. *¡Ay Dios Mío!* he roars at last. *Mi amor, mi amor.*

I run my dry lips over the arch of his eyebrow, now a caterpillar, now a sable brush.

He pulls my hands over my head, his thumbs digging shapes into my palms as if teaching words to the blind. *I let you get close and think that everything is normal, but if I wanted, you would see stars.*

The venom of my laughter.

True. He digs his thumbs in deeper. *Don't forget that.*

Only on the dance floor of course. The hiss of my own voice.

All the time. Everywhere. And for the rest of your life.

We speak with the forked tongues of reptiles, our bodies coiling around each other, waiting for sun to filter through the glass, warmth for our cold blood.

If the phone rings at seven thirty in the morning, it is usually my mother. If the phone rings at seven thirty in the morning on August 14, it is always my mother singing "happy birthday to you," sounding, as her voice does, like a poor man's version of Peggy Lee.

"Mom, that's amazing. You should take that show on the road." I stretch out spread-eagle in my too-big bed.

"I've decided you've got to start lying about your age, beginning now," she says. "You're making me look bad."

She asks what my plans are for today, and I list my "salsa theme," a dance class with Laura after a quick morning ride on Harley, dinner with my girlfriends at a chichi Cuban place in Hollywood called Paladar, and then out to see the salsa competition finals at the Conga Room.

"Are you dancing in them?" she asks.

"Hello? Are you high?"

"Well, I don't know. You've been taking these lessons for months now. I thought maybe you'd vastly improved."

"If only." I bemoan my lack of skill, explain how quickly I get confused with counting the beat and how I still often freeze up when I dance, filled with nervousness, but, paradoxically, how much I long to do it. It's the most perplexing experience of my life.

"You're too analytical, that's your problem. That's always been your problem," she says. "Don't think, just feel the music. Feel the floor."

I think of the times I saw her dancing in bars, the shake of her hips, the roll of her shoulders, and how embarrassed I used to feel as a kid at having such a sexy mom. She's told me of the night she met my father, the tight black dress she wore, the way she saw him across a room dancing with a blonde who had no rhythm, the way she caught his eye. And then they danced. I understand now what it must have been like, the two of them moving easily across the floor in unison, the exhilaration that had to spark.

"Tell me something," I begin, "what was the first song you ever danced to with my father?"

All my life, when I've asked her details about him, she's said that she doesn't remember or doesn't care, or that she never knew, but today she immediately breaks into:

> *Pretty woman*
> *walking down the street*

"He sang some words with his accent, then just hummed. When we went out after that, he always requested that song." Her voice sounds young, almost girlish. "That night we danced one more slow song, then went out to the parking lot—*to look at the moon*. Nothing else! Samantha, quit thinking what you're thinking."

I imagine them taking the floor, doing a smooth swing step, their hands hooked together. She would have been wearing that heavy perfume called Windsong, the one the ad promised would "stay on his mind." She would have felt his shoulder muscle under the blue Oxford shirt he wore, and he held her close enough for her breasts to brush his chest. Enchantment happened at that moment, some chemical reaction so intoxicating both of them felt the rush of it. When the music faded he asked her if she would care to step outside with him. Or maybe he didn't need to talk at all. Maybe he just held out his hand in offering.

I hereby discard the final vestige of respectability and enter a life of endless redress, into exile, leading to a land where sunset is always a scorched rind over a relentless blue. I will cry but never say I regret, because I'm going to know the rarest secret, the secret of having been loved so deep down in my marrow that even my teeth ache. That's what she's thinking when she takes his hand.

I imagine being her girlfriend, trying to talk her out of it, warning her, telling her about the shame and the struggle and the unhappiness that will spring from this one act. But no matter what I say, she takes his hand anyway.

"So I have Roy Orbison to thank for my birth?"

"In a manner of speaking."

"That's too cool."

She's quiet on the line for a moment. "Happy birthday, babydoll."

Ladies Styling

*Saturday Workshop taught by Laura Canellias,
one of the foremost instructors of Salsa in Los
Angeles! Emphasizes Cuban motion, turns,
and arm and hand styling. $12 or class card.*

Today, double spins.

I have to remind myself that I have requested this instruction of my own free will, sought it out in fact. It has not been imposed on me by some alien, oppressive regime that exists only to confirm that when it comes to all matters physical, I am constitutionally inferior.

But that's how it feels. I'm beginning to suspect my true nature is essentially bovine. That is to say blocky, unduly labored by the force of gravity, which, I have discovered, is not an impartial force (contrary to the prevailing scientific evidence) but rather a fickle, sadistic god randomly mandating who can move freely and who will suffer its weight.

J. and I have been chipping in for semiprivate lessons with
Laura in addition to the group dance classes. We are joined
by a twenty-something banker we met in Salsa II—I'll call
him Hector—who, despite his mild manner, has also been
infected with the salsa fever and is determined to get good
enough to wow people on the dance floor. And, oh yeah, he
happens to be from Belize. And, yes, he is six foot two and
absolutely gorgeous. But of course that had nothing to do
with our decision to agree to share our private lessons with
him. Honest.

Our lessons have moved downstairs from the main
dance studio to a small room called "the Holodeck," the studio owners being serious *Star Trek* fans. Previous renters
painted a mural of the solar system on the ceiling—so-called
psychics who read palms for five bucks but could not see the
end of their lease coming. The floors were already hard-
wood, so all the studio needed to do was add a barre and
full-length mirrors to the longest wall and, presto, more
room to practice.

I like this space, its celestial mood and blue tone, the
silly one-dimensional astronauts gazing down from a moon
shaped more like an egg. (Evidently the psychics were not
painters in any lifetime.) Usually there's something about
the room that makes me feel free, as if I'm again a girl
dancing for fun alone in my bedroom, the sound track to

Saturday Night Fever crackling from the turntable, bouncing on the trailer floor until the collection of Love's Baby Soft cologne bottles shakes off the built-in dresser shelf onto the shag throw rug, spilling a powdery scent. Having a lesson in this space station usually makes me revert to using words like *bitchin'*.

Not today. I feel irritated and self-conscious, and I seem to be the only one among us so bothered. J. wears a horizontal striped sundress with dorky Puma sneakers, her hair pulled up in a ratty bun stuck together by a chopstick, yet, somehow, she looks marvelous and yummy, like one of those big lollipops kids lick at the state fair. She practices hook turns quietly in the corner, her face set in concentration.

Hector, come straight from the office, has taken off his designer-labeled dress shirt and silk tie and now is down to the bone white of his cotton T-shirt. The material lies perfectly over the carved lines of his physique. His skin really is the color of walnuts. Hector seems always to be camera ready, like the Taj Mahal or some other wonder of the world—not trying to be spectacular, just stunningly, naturally so.

Me, I have on stretched-out yoga pants that keep riding down my hips, and wear a black bra under my wife-beater T-shirt, which, I've just noticed, has tiny orange juice stains running down the front. What I was thinking when I got dressed, I have no idea. Knots in my hair (dirtier than it looks) pull quietly at my scalp, and I kind of hate my two compadres at this moment.

Laura has just asked us to form three lines perpendicular to the mirror. Our goal is to complete four rotations so that we end up across the room, facing the same direction in which we started.

This is supposed to be accomplished by beginning with the right foot forward, arms out, not unlike the way birds extend their wings. To achieve motion, simply draw the left foot toward the right while folding the arms together, then open again, then close again. Or so it is in theory. If J. and Hector are swans, then I am the mechanical goose. My arms somehow remain cocked out and my shoulders hunch, and I end up with my back to the wall I'm supposed to be facing. There's something about this whole thing that's starting to remind me of junior high PE, the F I got for gymnastics.

"Let's partner up," Laura says finally, perhaps aware that I am about to throw a tantrum, adulthood be damned.

She pushes "play" on the stereo, and that crazy island rhythm pours out, drums and horns like a shot of some drug mainlined into my artery. The singer's Spanish words cry of *brujeria*, of witchcraft, of enchantment, and Hector takes my hands in his.

What is supposed to happen: he steps back on the fifth beat and raises his hand, bringing my arms over my head as I take a small forward step to push off, propelling me into a series of spins. Think of a dandelion twirled under his fingers. But I only get halfway around and collapse awkwardly, pulling his arms so that he too loses equilibrium.

I am the dandelion with the broken stem, wilting before the eye.

"Am I doing something wrong?" he asks me, concerned, biting the inside of his lip as he does when he's replaying a pattern in his head, looking for the movements he needs to hone, the beat he might have skipped.

I shake my head, wishing I could say, "Yes, it's you, damn it; you're in control of the dance; you have to make me better," but even though the man is responsible for creating the environment for the dance between the two partners, I can't say this. I'm the one who's not holding up my end. "No," I reassure him. "I'm just a cow."

"Switch," says Laura, who has been dancing with J.

Hector passes me off, and Laura holds my fingers, our steps moving in unison for a second before she leads me into the spin.

"I know what you're doing." She stops, puts a hand on her hip. "You're not trusting the man to help spin you; you're trying to spin all by yourself, and that is putting you off balance. Use him, girl! You're not supposed to do this all alone, you know."

I know she's taking about dancing, but what she is proposing implies a complete shift in my personal cosmology, like Copernicus saying the earth is revolving around a fixed sun. All at once I'm picturing being thirteen again at the Enchanted Hills Mobile Home Park, how we could have qualified for government housing. Consider: one single mother, sole supporter of both her daughter and her own mother on a nurse's wage. But thoughts of government housing would no more have entered Mom's head than running for president. A trailer might not have represented the kind of respectability my family wanted to project, but it was ours, hard-won, no man needed; there was pride in that. I'm imagining the look on my grandmother's face if she heard me say I needed a man to help me do anything, let alone spin me in a dance. A Good Man—one who would stay, have a job, and have not one other woman—was akin to a unicorn. Always secretly hoped for, heard tell of, but never, ever seen.

"Trust a man?" I say, the campy levity of my tone completely artificial, but necessary, like Sweet'N Low to cover the bitterness of coffee.

"I know, what a concept, right?" says Laura, and our eyes meet, our smiles not quite smiles.

"Hey, come on, Sam, you can trust me," Hector teases in a brotherly, offhand way.

I don't know if Laura has said to switch partners again, but suddenly Hector is there with his palm pressed to mine, my other hand resting on his arm as he holds my rib cage, the curve of his thumb finding a space between two ribs. The dance requires that I look up into his eyes, which are two points deep as the night with no stars. Then I imagine what trust would feel like, and sense that I am being rocketed into space, into a vastness for which I have no compass, and I am afraid.

Usually I don't pick up if I see the words *private number* flash on my phone's caller ID, because nine times out of ten it's a solicitation for something I don't need and would never buy, like a condominium, portable solar panels, or another newspaper subscription. Somebody must be buying things over the phone; otherwise this practice would shrivel up and die. But who? Who?

Well of course you know the answer: my mother.

My mother is the reason every single person in America is getting annoying phone calls. She alone gives solicitors hope.

I wait until the last ring before deciding on the spur of the moment to pick up the call. My friend Rachel's number registers as "private," and I think she might be calling to give me an update on her revolving boyfriend situation.

"Can I speak to Samantha, please?" The voice on the other end is sonorous, relaxed, male.

"This is she," I reply, using that professional voice I mentioned a while ago.

"Hi, Samantha. This is Carlos Gomez, the friend of Lauren's. Sorry it's taken me so long—"

Oh, my, my, my.

So this is Carlos Gomez. Doesn't sound like a loser dude at all. Sounds pretty promising in fact. You can tell right away. Then again, that envelope-making guy who talked about his ex-wife for three hours had sounded great on the phone, too. . . .

I'd tell you what we say here on the phone, but I really don't remember, and I don't have it written down anywhere. It's nice and pleasant, though, about being busy with work and the how-do-you-know-Lauren chitchat stuff. I do remember that. And I also remember we agree to meet that Thursday at the Spanish Kitchen, one of those chic places on the restaurant row of La Cienega, a famous artery of Los Angeles. All at once as I'm writing the address down I realize my Spanish classes are actually kicking in; after the eons I've lived here I think I might know what *la ciénega* means. It's "the marsh." But what marsh? Did there used to be a marsh where the road ended? It's all lost to the concrete now; only the words from the previous centuries remain.

Anyway, in the course of the conversation Carlos mentions, I think, that he looked up my books on the Internet. He also says he has a Web site. I make a note to check it when I have a moment. For now, though, I'm running to a late class with Laura, then to dinner with J., then we're going out dancing. Tonight, the Cock 'n Bull, a British pub in Santa Monica, kind of a dive on Lincoln Boulevard, but the hard-core mambo crowd migrates there every Tuesday organized by Mike "the Mambo Fello" Bello, a blue-eyed Puerto Rican transplanted from Brooklyn who is fervently evangelical in his desire to spread the mambo.

I'll end up going alone, as J.'s husband will not endorse the idea of his wife spending time after dark in an ill-lit club on a street better known for buying crack than any legitimate social endeavor. I'm at once thrilled and terrified of being among such serious dancers; it's like my own private horror movie every time I hear, "Like to dance?"

"Dancing is about creating lines," Laura tells us. Today her color is yellow, up to and including the scrunchy that pulls her long hair into a ponytail, like a sunburst in the center of the studio.

J. and I are on either side of her, facing the full-length mirror. When Hector can't join us, we concentrate the first twenty minutes of class on learning how to move our limbs gracefully, how to make an arm seem to float down as a feather might, how to roll a shoulder and have it look like a jaguar's motion, how to bend and straighten our knees so that the shock waves radiate up to make our hips sway.

I call this the "refeminization" process, and for me it feels like a radical act. Early in my life I got the message that all things girlic equaled soft, which equaled weak, and of course that's something I never, ever wanted to be. Perhaps, now that I think about it, it's more that softness was a luxury we could not afford. Now I'm finding a peculiar fulfillment in moving this way, like the feeling I had wearing that dress in New York, an unexpected surge of strength and a sense of equilibrium.

Laura is saying, "Think about your hands. Imagine that you're holding an orange in each of them." She holds her left arm out to the side, her other arm above her head. On each hand the tips of her middle finger and thumb touch lightly, and she does look like some image of an eastern goddess forming mudras with her hands, invoking powers from other realms. My eye is loath to leave her.

"Delicate, be very delicate. Think wet nails," she says. When this fails to provoke any change she explains, "Imagine you've just painted your fingernails and have to hold them out while they dry."

Laura smiles broadly at us. "Now, girls, let's do a little salsa housekeeping." She tells us we're going to pull together all the hand, hip, and foot action we've been practicing, then she puts on a groovy Cuban tune called "La Negra Tiene Tumbao" by Celia Cruz. (If you're a *salsera*, you're crossing yourself right now and saying "God rest her soul" in whatever language you know, because Celia Cruz is revered to the point of divinity.)

"Attention, divas-in-training! Tits out, ass out, fingernails wet!" Laura checks our posture in the mirror. "Pretend *he's* coming over tonight—and you know what I mean—so what are you going to do? That's right, clean the house! Now take your arms up and *flick* that box on the closet shelf! Take your foot and *kick* that dirt under the bed! Take your hip and *bump* the couch! Now *smooth* the sheets on the bed! Keep the count, girls, we're working on the two today! One-TWO-three, five-SIX-seven. Again! One-TWO-three, five-SIX-seven . . ."

Miraculously J. and I, together with Laura, form a somewhat respectable trio, creating a mini salsa burlesque right there in front of the mirror. It seems I have never laughed so hard or felt so—what is the word?—*normal*. I feel normal. And hopeful. If Anne Sullivan could teach Helen Keller to speak, Laura Canellias can teach me to dance.

Pearl S. Buck, the same Pearl S. Buck who won the Nobel Prize for Literature, by all evidence an accomplished, brilliant woman, fell completely nuts for her Arthur Murray dance teacher in Pittsburgh, a guy half her age named Ted Harris. She was so taken with Teddy, with whom she took up ballroom lessons in her dotage, that she left him her fortune. Of course her family had something to say about that in court; they reasoned that he had to have taken advantage of her, connived, swindled. Evidently they didn't consider that maybe dear old Teddy merely had the foresight to treat Pearl not like a literary legend but as if she were still a woman who could hope and who could love, which of course is exactly what she was. No doubt Ted Harris made her feel that she was seen, when most everyone else looks past an eighty-year-old woman as if she were a tree or a rock.

"A lot of women get a thing for their dance teachers, you know, because when you dance you break that boundary of personal space," says Jacob, or I'll call him Jacob anyway. "We touch them in a way only their families or lovers or their pets ever do. Things get confused sometimes."

Is Jacob telling me this just to make conversation, or do I have the I-already-slept-with-my-instructor logo tattooed on my forehead? Jacob is one of these rare, original mambo guys from the East Coast who'll recall the time they saw Tito jam with Machito at the Palladium, tell you how many steps you had to climb to get to the entrance (eighteen), and give you the feel of how to cha-cha right (on two) like only old Jewish guys can. Picture Jacob, God knows how old he really is, who is fit and trim and moves as if on a greased axle, with the Grecian Formula hair and the immaculately starched white shirt buttoned to the top, the face that looks incapable of surprise. He gargles Drakkar Noir.

At this point I have a lot of time to talk to Jacob when I go out dancing, because he's a retired instructor, third generation, ballroom style, and he does not ever dance with beginners. (You're considered a beginner if you've been dancing less than a year and/or have no ability.) Never. Not ever. Only Laura and maybe, *maybe*, a handful of other serious *salseras* are sought by Jacob.

"I did my time. I don't do community service. I only want to have fun," he explains, even though I don't ask for any justification for not being asked (although I might look a little wistful when I hear that Jimmy Bosch trombone on one song).

Of course he's far from the only potential partner, but I've reached a kind of purgatory in my social dancing. I'm still new enough that good dancers don't recognize me, so will give me one dance, at which point they realize how novice, that is, bad I am, so they don't ask me again. Other bad dancers will ask me a few times, but it's excruciating for both of us. Great dancers, those glitter jewels, are the Brahmin caste of salsa society, and no matter if my cleavage is served on a golden platter and my newly slim midriff is naked as truth, they are not going to waste one dance on an untouchable beginner. I've figured out these Brahmin types are essentially junkies who've crossed over into mainlining. For them salsa is beyond feelings of connection and enjoyment. They're chasing that perfect dance, the ultimate hit, nirvana at their feet. They don't care who supplies it. They just want to make sure they get it.

(The exception to the Brahmin-versus-Untouchable situation is the time a true *salsero* decides he wants your phone number, and will dance repeatedly with you until he gets it; at which point he will return to dancing with his caste. Then you'll go out with him and have the predictable hot-and-heavy thing, because what have your dances been but extended foreplay? And how often does a woman get true foreplay, really? However, this liaison will turn out to have the duration of a bacterial infection and about as much emotional significance. It will burn out quick as a paper fire, after which you'll avoid each other in the clubs until you both forget what your thing was about in the first place, then occasionally try another awkward dance together, and, finally, owing to sheer lack of interest, avoid each other completely.)

Anyhow, I spend a lot more time at tables and on barstools at this point, talking to Jacob and watching the spontaneous floor show that erupts wherever *salseros* congregate, than actually dancing myself.

"You got to know that you can't confuse the dancer with the person," Jacob is explaining in a loud voice. "When you meet the dancer, you're meeting what moves them, and how they experience beauty. But that doesn't mean you know how they operate in the world or if they have integrity. Maybe some guy can dance like a dream but be a killer."

The air in the Cock 'n Bull is sticky with perspiration and the wet slap of drinks hitting the bar. Couples move on the floor; the damp intertwine of their bodies mesmerizes me, the throb of *tumbao* and clack of the claves incarnated by their flesh. I have to be honest about this: knowing who someone is as a dancer feels to me to be the truest, most exalted statement of his essential nature. I want to experience other people at the point where their highest yearning and joyous expression intersect with their most primal instincts. This, to me, is the essence of salsa.

What are you going to do when you get back home at two in the morning—rooms empty of life save for a huge, snoring dog and lots of plants that need water—except Google Carlos Gomez? I can't find the verb *to Google* anywhere in my *Unabridged Random House Dictionary of the English Language,* but it's an old edition. The editors must have updated it to include this listing, meaning "to scour the Internet with the Google search engine, usually late at night, for information about a person who's piqued your interest."

A few keystrokes later, I sit in front of the screen, gaping like a fish pulled out of water.

The dark hair. The wise, sad eyes. This must be a publicity photo from some movie where he played a cop, because he looks tough.

Carlos Gomez is the same guy who stopped the earth's orbit at the Los Van Van concert. The one I searched for in the crowd, the one I didn't find.

A sign. A big fat freeway sign from God.

What are the odds? I didn't even mention the Los Van Van mystery man episode to Lauren—not that it would have provided any worthwhile information anyway. Clearly, this coincidence is an omen of something.

Now might be a good time to confess my predilection toward the occult, hocus-pocus, woo-woo stuff, call it what you will. It's not something I'm especially proud of, seeing as I would like to be considered a person who is, if not intellectual, then at least rational. However, this is an ingrained part of my personality, so I might as well "own it," as the expression goes. I inherited the Gaelic tendency to be superstitious from my mother's side, and certainly some Italian something was passed through my father's genetic coding, all of which has been convoluted and magnified over the years by being raised in New Mexico, land of Native American mysticism and spooky Catholicism. (Have a problem? Mrs. Garcia next door says hold your statue of la Virgen hostage by burying her in the yard until you get what you want! Need a boyfriend? Hang Saint Anthony upside down and watch your *novio* appear!) Living in California has further exacerbated my susceptibility. I'm friendly with two professional astrologers and have been known to consult pet psychics regarding Harley's emotional well-being.

Truth is, I essentially live as people did in the Dark Ages anyway. Looking at the world around me, I don't understand how any of what I depend on for survival is formed or why it operates. Computer, car, cell phone, hybrid apples. Of course I recognize words like *binary code* and *genetic engineering* and *ions* and for that matter *electricity*, but it might as well all arrive on fairy wings for as much as I comprehend about how the tangible reality is actually created. In this age of subatomic physics and space travel, it doesn't seem such a stretch to also consider that chanting a mantra might correct negative karma. Says me.

I eat my meals in the kitchen with Nacha, where we watch Spanish-language news programs on television, which, I have to say, acknowledge and value the mystical in modern life in a way English-language programs would never consider (or at least I guess the Spanish shows do, since I only understand about a third of what is said). These programs feature global news, celebrity gossip, financial updates, sports, and political commentary right alongside "Walter y Las Estrellas" (Walter and the Stars). Walter is a blond bon vivant who favors purple caftans and large, shimmering jewelry, who not only gives daily astrological predictions but reads the tarot, dispenses homeopathy cures, and dabbles in feng shui. If I skip a day, Nacha is sure to give me updates; Sunday mass and daily Walter are two things she never misses.

I search for a reference to Carlos's birth date on the Internet, because in the morning I'll tell Nacha all about this fortuitous event, and she will have to know his sign so she can start tracking him via Walter.

I find it: January. That makes him a Capricorn.

My mother is a Capricorn. My grandmother was, too.

Hmm.

Spins and Turns Workshop

Drill the fundamentals of these essential maneuvers:

Good review for levels I and II. Sign-ups through Friday. $12 or class card.

L et's say it's a cloudless Tuesday in late August, another afternoon when I'm finding it hard to sit in front of my computer. The phone rings, and, lo and behold, what do I hear on the other end of the line but, "Babe, hey. It's me. You still in New York?"

"I haven't been there in a month."

"No way, really? Man, time flies."

Don't think I don't know he's pretending, or doing what would be called in dancing a "fake out," where you create the appearance that you're going in one direction but really moving in another. He knows damn well I'm not in his town, which makes it safe to call me, because nothing will be required of him. However, I'm feeling benevolent. I'm going out with Carlos Gomez tonight, which surely means that everything in my life is about to become perfect. Nacha agrees the signs are everywhere. If my *former* dance instructor wants to be a weasel, I can afford to be forgiving.

Turns out he'll be here next month for some performances. I'm not sure if he's contacting me because he wants to sleep with me or to ensure he has at least one private student lined up so he can make some money. But what am I thinking? In his perfect world he'll be sleeping with me *and* I'll be giving him money.

Well, forget that. By next month Carlos Gomez and I might be madly in love, and I'll be too busy.

Then again, there is no one I enjoy dancing with more. Maybe it's that he was my first *salsero* and you always have a soft spot for your first, or it could be that he truly is one of the most splendid salsa dancers on the planet.

Or both.

Suddenly the thought of dancing with him makes me excited. It's not sex—that you can get anywhere—but the anticipation of his fantastic lead that gives me butterflies. I am nervous envisioning dancing with him; after all these months I feel I should be better than I am. I blurt this out.

He replies, "Can I ask you, do you have fun when you dance with me?"

"What kind of a question is that?"

"Just tell me, do you have fun?"

"You know I do." Why am I being sucked into this conversation? I think of the old *Wonder Woman* television show and the golden lasso she used to tie around people to make them spontaneously burst into truth-telling. "Dancing with you is what got me hooked on this whole deal in the first place."

It sounds like he's eating cereal while talking on the phone; I hear the smack and crunch over the receiver. "So ask yourself, 'If I'm having fun, what the fuck do I care what anybody else thinks?'"

He's right. I spent the early part of my thirties hobbled, a candidate for amputation, and now I dance for hours. Pain or no pain, I do it. I hate that he's right. Now is the time to change the subject.

"It was completely rude of you not to call before," I say in what I think is an offhand way. "Especially after the Holiday Inn."

"Babes, you got to understand, I just moved back here, and it's crazy. I'm trying to get some big things going. There's a lot of pressure." This is an interesting tone; it might be sincerity, I'm not sure. "I can understand how when I didn't call you'd think it meant something bad. But I didn't mean it like that. Baby. Hey. C'mon."

Then I tell him, Well, OK, but you're still an ass, and he says, I know, lamb chop. I'm really sorry. Then I don't say anything at all, and he says, Why have you got to be far like that? I hate it when you're far like that.

My literal date with Destiny.

This requires wardrobe approval from J., who votes for the low-slung Brazilian-cut embroidered jeans, the bronze V-neck sleeveless top, and those strappy beige heels she bequeathed me. The look: sexy, but not slutty; glam, but not dressy. Clothes in fact were the easy part. It was everything else that took forever: hair ironed straight, pedicure, manicure for the new nails I'm growing under Laura's influence. I even wash my cruddy mini SUV in case he sees me pull up. (In the regional idiom of Los Angeles, the word for *parking lot* is *valet*.)

But then I get stuck in traffic on Sunset Boulevard. Where are all these people going on a Thursday night? Have they no homes, no lives?

I'm to meet him at eight o'clock. It's ten to eight.

Then it's five to eight.

I call the restaurant. Beg the hostess to get a message to a handsome Latino named Carlos Gomez that his date is on her way. Hang up. Realize telling somebody to find a handsome Latino named Carlos Gomez in Los Angeles at the Spanish

Kitchen is like telling her to find a tree in a forest. Panic and call back. Breathe a sigh of relief when she says, "Yes, I found the right one, and he says, 'No problem, take your time.'"

Picture this: fitted jeans, loose T-shirt, boots, a glass of sangria in hand. He's about two inches taller than I am. He greets me in that European hello way with a kiss on the cheek. "Nice to meet you. I'm Carlos."

He has a clean, just-showered scent, and his cheek is smooth from a shave. And I'll tell you right here, he's everything I hoped he would be.

A gentleman? Oh, don't you know that he pulls the seat out for me at our corner table. Asks me my preferences, orders for us.

Sex appeal? Our hands brush as we both reach for our drinks, and I feel that shiver of attraction. It was his idea to share a dessert, which suggests sexual temptation, according to a magazine article I think I wrote once.

Charming? Are you kidding? One word: dimples.

Smart? If he's not, he sure can fake it.

Sense of humor? He laughs at my jokes, which indicates something, if only that he's courteous.

Things in common? He took salsa lessons from Laura! And I tell him about seeing him at the Los Van Van concert, a coincidence that obviously implies oh so much. He remembers the concert but, well, does not remember seeing me.

We spend three hours talking. All right, that's an over-statement. Likely it's just two and change. And maybe I'm nervous because I seem to be doing a lot of talking. In fact I don't recall much of what he says. I do know that I am happy having a wonderful evening with a wonderful man and feeling like wonderful suits me just fine.

I'm going to say it's a hot night, one of those Santa Ana evenings when the sky stays a deep indigo and never turns fully black. People swarm the sidewalk waiting to get inside the restaurant; bumper-to-bumper car lights brighten the street, an unbroken line of white and red and yellow like some metallic coral snake. The valet quickly pulls my car up after Carlos gives him the ticket.

"This you?" Carlos points to my car with the missing sideview mirror and the bent fender. It is, however, clean.

"You could say."

Carlos engulfs me in a warm embrace for a brief moment, and he kisses my cheek for the second time this evening. "This was so much fun," he says.

"For me too. Thanks for a great evening." I tip the valet and give Carlos that superwattage Farrah smile while I try to think of a good way to ask him if he wants to grab a nightcap somewhere else. But I don't need to bother.

"It was a blast meeting you," he's saying pleasantly as another valet comes with his car. "Take care of yourself, and keep in touch!"

Keep in touch.

That's when I know I'll never hear from Carlos Gomez again.

"Well?" My mother couldn't wait until seven-thirty in the morning; she has to call at eleven o'clock to hear the play-by-play on my encounter with Destiny. "I can't believe you're home already. I thought you'd be out salsa-ing or doing who knows what with Carlos Gomez."

"It wasn't like that," I say. "It was fantastic. And I'm never going to hear from him again."

I rewind the evening for her, then give my analysis of the "keep in touch" ending.

She concurs. "Yeah, he's a goner. What can I say? You win some, you lose some."

All at once I feel maudlin, overwhelmed in a quicksand of self-pity. When am I going to get this dating thing right? "This would have been a nice one to win," I say.

"You're looking at it the wrong way," she tells me. "Finally you had a date with someone who wasn't a loser. Take that as your minimum standard from now on. Shoot for a Carlos Gomez or above."

"I don't go out with losers, Mother!" Damn but she pisses me off.

"You always go out with losers. With a capital *L*."

"According to the prevailing psychotherapeutic theories, children form their relationship models from the parental behavior they observe." Why am I on the phone with her at this hour? I just want to put on my pajamas and go to bed. For a week.

"What, exactly, is your point?"

"Glass house. Stone throwing."

She sighs. The deep exhale causes a brief spasm of coughing. "I just want to see you with someone who treats you the way you deserve to be treated. Somebody who understands how precious you are. That's all."

We are both quiet for what feels like a long time. "Thank you, Mom," I say finally. "I hear what you're telling me."

"Good night, pussycat."

L.A. Style

*Learn the flashy tricks of
Hollywood's hottest
"on one" rumberos!
Monday class through
November free with $5 cover!
Two-drink minimum. Sorry, no passes.*

People I know from before salsa, they all have their opinions.

Spencer from the Zen Center, a bodhisattva by way of Brooklyn: "I don't know about this salsa thing. You must have fucked more Cubans than Castro by now." (I assure him they're not all Cuban.)

Anita from Caracas, in my writing workshop: "What is it with you and Latin men? I could just slap you! You know what a Venezuelan woman means when she says, 'I got a good one'? It means she married an American. Snap out of it!"

Bruce, fellow instructor at the university: "I don't want to say anything, but this relates back to your father issues. I can give you a therapist's number if you want. . . ."

Edward is the only person who can truly understand my conversion to the merits of wearing body glitter and the hunger to be on a dance floor. He was the one who saw my left leg all but hacked off from my body, which is why he never questions the current routine of daily dance classes, the almost nightly schedule of clubs.

"When we were waiting for the paramedics to find us, all of a sudden you asked me why you didn't dance. Do you remember that?" I see him today at the barn, and he puts an arm around my shoulder.

I nod.

"And do you remember I swore to you that you'd dance? And you looked at me like I was crazy?" He grins.

"In my defense, consider the circumstances," I say, giving him a big hug.

"Believe me now?"

For years, Sundays would begin with a morning meditation at the Zen Center, followed by an afternoon ride, then probably a yoga class, ending with an evening of HBO. Now

Sundays begin with an afternoon ride, because getting up before eleven has become impossible. At this point on any given Sunday evening I will be found sitting among the coven of *salseras* at Laura's table at the Sagebrush in Culver City, a large Mexican restaurant that becomes the epicenter of the L.A. salsa scene every weekend. It is soon to fade into local legend because new owners are taking it over, but none of the hundreds who dance here know this yet; even Laura and her partner, famed salsa promoter Albert Torres, who put on the event every week, are oblivious as to the eventual fate of the Sagebrush.

My two *comadres* (that means compadres in skirts) at the table are debating the value of dancing on the classic two as opposed to the New York two, or "modern mambo." Clelia, a quick-tongued Venezuelan with onyx-colored eyes (and a body so shapely she could have been a center-fold if she wasn't an accountant with a master's degree from USC), seems again to be outtalking Veronica of the long, manelike brown hair and apricot skin, a preschool teacher and lifelong dance aficionado. I try to follow the discussion but lose interest. I had no idea there was so much math in salsa.

I'm feeling like I have too much cherry lipstick and not enough Botox, but I can't make myself go home. I need a little Eddie Palmieri, some Celia Cruz, a round of "Oye Como Va" would do. Anything to assuage the unbearable whiteness of being. I eye the dozens of couples whirling around one another, hoping to spot a nice lead, a sure thing, one I already know.

"Dance?" A man who must be barely old enough to drink legally offers me his hand; he has the copper skin and high cheekbones of many who are native to Peru, and in fact he turns out to be from Lima. I know this because I nervously ask my partners questions as we take the floor, hoping this will distract them from trying anything too complicated.

It doesn't work this time, as he soon tries to shoot me into a series of right spins. I, however, have my elbow cocked out too far and clock him across the jaw so hard his head whips back and he loses balance for a second.

For a moment I feel like I'm having a flashback to 1992, in the mosh pit again as the band Ministry plays at the Lollapalooza festival, feeling revved up by the assault of sound coming from the stage. Then I remember where I am. "Oh, god, I'm so, so sorry!" I exclaim, stopping to put my hands on his shoulders. "Are you all right?"

He looks at me like I'm something he needs a holy cross to ward off. Not only have I humiliated him by belting him on a dance floor, but now I'm bringing attention to it. Even if he were being chased by wolves, he couldn't return me to my seat and vanish into the crowd any faster.

"Back so soon?" Clelia asks.

"Girls," I begin, mortified to confess my latest blunder on the floor, far worse than the usual stomping of toes, the missed hands for the lead, the wobbly turns, the chronic stepping on the wrong beat. I expect them to be equally shocked, but nary an eyelash is batted.

"It was his own fault," says Veronica. "He was too close and probably didn't prepare you."

"It happens." Laura shrugs. "One night at Rudolfo's a girl knocked her partner's teeth out, I mean all over the dance floor. And at least he finished the dance. That's what a real *salsero* does."

Somebody else says, "What was that guy doing putting his face in the way of your dancing anyway?"

Still, I mope and try to smother my embarrassment with a plate of cheese enchiladas. Jacob comes to sit next to me at an adjoining table. "What's a matter?"

I tell him of my "combat salsa" maneuver. "I should have started dancing when I was a kid. Now it's hopeless," I complain.

"No, that's where you're wrong." He leans forward and looks me in the eye. "It's really a good thing you waited until you were in your thirties to start dancing, I'm telling you. When you start dancing young, yeah, it's better in terms of training physical reflex, but it's all about sex. Sex, and ego. When you're older, it's more about self-expression. It's about"—he touches the front of his pressed white shirt—"the heart."

At this time there are really only four places in L.A. proper I know of that offer salsa as the mainstay of their business: the Cuban restaurant El Floridita in Hollywood, the Conga Room on the Miracle Mile of Wilshire Boulevard, the tapas bar Mama Juana's in Studio City, and Rudolfo's nightclub in Silverlake. Otherwise, salsa places are kind of like speakeasies, usually held in back of or on the off nights of different establishments that normally have little or nothing to do with Latin music. The hard-core aficionados number about two hundred and follow the same circuit week after week, even though the circuit stretches across an area that's about the size of Luxembourg: Mondays, El Floridita or Rudolfo's; Tuesdays, there's the Cock 'n Bull; Wednesdays, the Polynesian restaurant Monsoon in Santa Monica, or the Marriot in the South Bay; Thursdays, Steven's Steakhouse in the City of Industry; Fridays, Sportsman's Lodge. Sundays, as previously mentioned, the Sagebrush.

My first few times at the Sagebrush, I check out the good-looking men, hoping they'll ask me to dance so I can get a rush off their testosterone. I will admit that in the back of my mind there is the thought that, perhaps, one may be a Carlos Gomez.

But after several weeks I increasingly find myself looking more at the broader picture created by how well a man moves, how happy other women seem dancing with him, how respectful he is of salsa etiquette. For example, the convention has it that he lead you politely by the hand to the floor and return you to where he found you, whenever possible. And no matter how sensuous the dance moves become, groping, kissing, or rubbing a hard-on against your partner is more than déclassé; it is unforgivably insulting. At the Sagebrush such behavior will quickly get the offender a "meeting" with Albert Torres's security team, Dave and Fernando. It is expected that the dance will be used as seduction—although much more rarely than the casual observer must imagine happens—but overt make-out sessions and crude displays by either partner are seriously frowned upon. This is because such behavior is a threat to the dance itself. Salsa provides a space separate, a sort of theater for sensual expression, a form that allows everyone to finally convey sexuality, desire, and passion safely, without judgment or repercussions.

Ultimately you might not be able to recognize your partner in a police lineup, but you do know intimately the texture of his palm and the curve of his fingers. A truly excellent salsa dancer, one who gives off the street grit that makes the hair on the back of your neck stand up, is not unlike a great pool player. It's the kind of skill achieved only after years spent in dark places.

I'm trying to understand why I'm not getting this. I mean really getting this. I have never in my entire life excelled at any physical endeavor—in truth I've never actually hungered

to be excellent at anything at all, apart from my work—
which begs the question of why this particular failure is
getting to me. Even as an equestrian I'm considered to have
an average, workman skill, not especially talented. Dancing
is different. I watch serious *salseras*, and I ache to know that
kind of movement within my own body; it's as if a part of me
knows it will unearth something long buried. Sure, by now
I can respectably manage basic patterns and can find the first
beat of music *most* of the time. I'm putting basic sentences
together—"How are you? I am fine. The weather is nice
today"—but it's like parroting phrases from a Berlitz
guidebook while all around me dancers are reciting poetry
to one another with their bodies.

It's not just that I'm neurotic. My partners get frustrated with me, too.

"No, turn the other way, *other* way, when I do that,"
says Enrique.

"Your 'bad' leg is bothering you? I thought they were
both your bad legs," says Phil.

"*Mira*, if the two of us try to drive the car, we get in an
accident. Leave the driving to me," says Julio.

Albert Torres himself asks for a dance; he stands only
five foot eleven but is the type who seems much taller, a bear
of a man. It can be said he resembles a hybrid between baseball player Sammy Sosa and the puppet Fozzy Bear. There's
a lumbering, cuddly quality to him, yet you're always aware
that with one swipe he could easily take somebody's head
off, and no doubt has, and doesn't mind that he has. I'd like

to say that the fear of dancing with salsa's biggest promoter, former professional dancer, and ex-con is what freezes
my reactions and turns my ear to tin, but this happens no
matter who's leading me.

"You get too worried. Just relax." He wraps his big
hands on my hips to steer me side to side, up and back. All
the gray through his wavy black hair gives it a sheen like
steel. "One day this is just going to click, and then you'll
have it for the rest of your life. I promise you."

Most of the communication in dance is of course not ver-
bal. Entire conversations are conducted through pressure
and touch and momentum and sight and a shift of weight. I
know men are speaking to me in this physical language, but
I'll be damned if I can make out a full sentence, even
a phrase. One by one, they stop asking me to dance. Entire
nights will go by, and not a hand will be extended in my
direction.

I'm contemplating giving up. Never mind that by this
point I have spent upward of three thousand dollars on lessons, devoted at least ten hours a week to this endeavor, have
been seen in public in a dress. *Salsa suicide. Just get it over
with. Walk out. Don't show up. Use those salsa CDs as coasters
for drinks. Quit. Burn the dance shoes J. gave you. End it all.
Don't leave a note.* Yet, somehow, somewhere, my despair is
observed, and mercy is delivered unto me in the form of:

Saint Errol.

It's all right if you haven't heard of him. Neither has the pope. I guess, technically, Errol could only be canonized after death, and then only if at least three separate miracles that occurred as a result of pleas for his intercession could be documented. And, I suppose, going strictly by the letter, he would need to be Catholic.

These are mere details, however. Belief doesn't need any paperwork. My mom still sends prayers to Saint Christopher, even though he's long since been booted from the canon; all over the world there are altars to local saints whose names are not on any roster in the Vatican. I therefore feel justified in adding my own: Saint Errol, patron of hapless *salseras* and the rhythmically challenged everywhere.

I don't really know how to describe Errol. The usual stats would help, I suppose: he's black, about six foot one, stocky build, large round eyes, and a baby's full cheeks. He's always casually dressed, in T-shirts and jeans, and smells clean in an Ivory soap way. Errol could be twenty-five, he could be fifty; it's impossible to tell. He exudes a politeness so profound it seems to be part of his cellular structure and not just something drilled into him as a cadet at the Air Force Academy. Errol has never been observed picking up women (or anybody else for that matter), asking for phone numbers, or trying any of the umpteen seductions even the most upright of *salseros* occasionally engage in. He's a fantastic dancer, a true Brahmin who, from all evidence and eyewitness accounts, really does hold the music and the dance above anything.

The first time he takes my hand, I give the usual disclaimer about my ability, which I've repeated so often now it sounds like the mumble at the end of the commercials for one of those prescription medications you're supposed to ask for by name.

Errol just nods, as if these facts are already known to him, and takes me in a close embrace—not seductively, just to prevent me from moving too largely and getting off beat. He contains me, as it were, within his own rhythm, giving me support. He doesn't instruct or guide; in fact, he says nothing at all. He just lets me feel the even, steady movement of his body, so comforting it is like listening to the ocean or to a heartbeat, lulling me into a deep feeling of security. When I step on his toes, there is no hint of frustration or disappointment. He merely smiles, stops, and starts us over again. Saint Errol embodies that essence I first sensed in the Conga Room, salsa at its highest expression: acceptance.

Every one of the dozens of dances I will later share with Errol are exactly this wonderful. There are nights when I go out only to get a dance with Errol, and then return home. For me these dances are as gratifying as riding Harley; silent, but more full of communication than if a thousand words were spoken.

There I am, I'm buying fresh carrots for Harley and a Gatorade for me at Gelson's Market in the Pacific Palisades.

Gelson's is the kind of grocery store that proclaims, "Rich White People Live in This Neighborhood." Psychedelic colors radiate from the produce section, with perfect little pyramids of imported apples, and exotic fruits like kumquats and guava displayed under lighting usually reserved for movie stars. The deli section offers cheeses from France and real foie gras. Outside, the parking lot could be mistaken for a Range Rover dealership. I leave my fine piece of Korean engineering on the street because the urban safari vehicles of my fellow shoppers crowd all the parking spaces.

The "Qwick Check" line of ten items or less, cash only, is of course the slowest line at the store, so there I stand in my paddock boots and dirty jeans, bored, staring blankly at the queue of people in front of me. I'm vaguely aware of a medley of sounds, the click of metal wheels from passing carts, the bleep of the electronic register, the flat drone of voices over an intercom, the mishmash of words surrounding me.

But I feel an odd sensation of something being different.

I look around. No, still the same Gelson's. Nothing has been remodeled. Same clerks. Same bag boys. Same interchangeable parade of blond housewives with unbelievably talented plastic surgeons. So, what is it? Why do I feel something has changed?

Then I realize that I'm understanding everything being said around me without effort or concentration. The checkout girl is telling the bag boy that her feet hurt; the bagboy is saying that this customer can never figure out how to use the ATM payment machine; the manager wants to know who needed the price check on toothpaste; the guy with a cart of lettuce is complaining he didn't get Saturday off last week. Nothing particularly exciting, for sure, but the thing is, I realize none of it is being said in English.

The cumulative effect of the Spanish classes, the daily salsa music, the brief but frequent conversations with dance partners from Latin American countries, and the TV viewing with Nacha has come together in this moment. It's as if the whole time I have lived in Los Angeles I have been watching a movie, following the plot, occasionally aware of things being a bit out of focus, but never bothering to put on those glasses with the blue-and-red plastic lenses handed out for free at the theater. Now I've put them on, and suddenly, the picture in front of me is full of new color and richness, a three-dimensional experience of action and intrigue that has been playing before my eyes all along.

The people working in the store are all Latino; almost all the customers, Anglo. The workers speak in Spanish to one another and in English to the customers. Meanwhile, the customers speak English all the way around, seemingly as oblivious as I have been to the fullness of life in front of us.

I have heard Mexican-Americans jokingly refer to *la reconquista*, to the West becoming once again a Spanish-speaking province. I can see some people shaking their heads, a cold little wash of terror down their spines, saying, "All the more reason to stop 'em at the border, damn it!" But just look at the census numbers: in Los Angeles, Latinos—the blanket term that covers such a wide range of people with different histories and races but who have in common the Spanish language—already constitute 45 percent of the population. It's too late, *amigo*. They are us now.

Yet we are also them. I think of the salsa I listen to, the steps I dance, and know that it is art that could only have been made by immigrants rubbing up against what they found here. Who knows what kind of culture we are going to end up with in fifty years? My bet is that we will be essentially the same, but maybe we'll eat a little spicier, maybe speak more than one language like Europeans do, maybe dance more often. We'll definitely be a little browner. I'm reminded of a quote from the critic Leslie Fiedler, who once said, "When two cultures meet, they sometimes make war. They always make love."

On my way out of Gelson's, I run into a clerk on a cigarette break and the store security guard who are inadvertently blocking the walkway as one tells the other about his daughter's baptism.

"*Con permiso,*" I say hesitantly.

They step out of the way, and both smile broadly. "*Por favor, pase usted, señora,*" replies the guard.

Advanced New York on 2

Perfect your N.Y. timing with Sportsman's Lodge Competition Champion and choreographer Raul Santiago! In town this week only!

I n December, the day after a blizzard, I am wading through a snowdrift with a suitcase from the curb to the door of his apartment in Queens. It began with a casual exchange on the computer's instant-message system:

Him: When are you coming out here?

I thought about it. I go to New York often but had no immediate plans. In theory I always have business I *should* be doing in the city to further my career: chatting up important editors for assignments, reminding my publisher of my existence, having my agent buy lunch, visiting friends, buying counterfeit Prada on street corners.

Me: Maybe in a couple weeks.

Him: Good. Stay with me. I miss you, babes.

Me: You say that to all your girls.

Him: Not even most.

Me: Can we have a dance lesson?

Him: If you ask nice.

Never mind the fact that this is right before Christmas, that I have about four hundred dollars in my checking account, that every meeting I have in New York could just as easily be done over the phone. Harley's fine with a few days off, I have no imminent deadlines, and no exciting plans for the immediate future. I impulsively buy a cheap ticket on a red-eye for a long weekend.

A man with a gold-tooth smile is shoveling snow off the stoop of the brick building. He identifies himself proudly as Angelo-the-Manager, as if the whole phrase is his christened name. He seems surprised to see a woman in black leather boots arrive at his building from a Lincoln towncar.

"Who ya here for?" he asks.

I hesitate, realizing that I have never said these words even to myself. "Raul," I say more quietly than I intended, so quietly he asks me to speak up. "I'm here for Raul Santiago."

I don't think I'm imagining the double take he gives me when I tell him, but Angelo recovers quickly. "I'll help you inside," he offers, leaving the shovel on the stoop.

At the top of the stairs I see an orange parka, blue jeans, and a newsboy cap. The imprint from creases in the bedsheet still patterns his face. What dancers do during the day is sleep, much like cats.

"Hey," he says, voice sleepy or maybe suddenly shy. He moves to take my bag, but I've overpacked (as always) and I worry that it might weigh too much for him to get down the stairs without an awkward struggle. I hand him my briefcase instead. "Here."

He shrugs and leads us down the stairs to open the door of his apartment. "Welcome to my humble home."

I look around the room. A kitchenette lines one corner; in the other stands his large glass-top desk and all his space-age music synthesizers and computer. The furnishings consist of a large futon, a dresser, a coffee table, and one reclining chair. His home is as neat and ordered as his clothes. Much like his dancing, actually. Nothing cluttered.

We have not even kissed hello, and he is pulling off his clothes, naked underneath the parka and jeans. "Come to bed. I'm so sleepy," he says as he jumps onto the futon and buries himself under the covers.

My first minute and a half at this address in Queens is spent stripping my clothes down to my underwear, which I briefly consider removing but then think that might come across as too forward, and besides, this turquoise is the one pair of expensive La Perla stuff I own, and it would be a shame if it didn't get noticed.

So I get under the covers, and he puts an arm around me. The bed is warm; I feel his muscles relax like a sleeping animal. The only sound is the regular, soft inhale of his breath. I too try to relax, willing myself to sleep, but I'm keyed up from the trip. I can't stop the rapid thud of my heart, which beats so loudly I think it might wake him. I repeat a few lines of a calming yoga mantra in my head, then wonder if hallowed words will work in this scenario.

We must doze, because I'm awakened by his hand at my waist. Then he groans, more like a slight growl, and I feel him move against me, pulling my hips tighter against his. His kisses then fall over my shoulders like snowflakes, his cool mouth, and he bites me gently on the arm. He moves a hand to my thighs, grabbing the heaviness that remains there, and then to my stomach, pressing his palm to the softness of it. "I love this," he murmurs.

"I'm too flabby," I say reflexively.

"You're perfect; you've always been perfect." He says this in such a way that, God help me, I believe he really does mean it.

I turn over to lie flat on my back, and he continues to kiss me, moving his hands to pull down the straps of my very expensive blue bra, which soon gets tossed out of the bed as an unwelcome accessory. He slips one finger along the ridge of the matching silk underpants.

"I thought you wanted to sleep," I pretend to object, spurred by some stunted attempt at modesty.

"What do you think?" he says before slipping the panties off me in one quick move.

Then there is that rhythm between us, him praying to every deity he knows and me kissing his neck, his shoulders, wrapped around him like a kind of perfumed vine.

Afterward we lie side by side. He gets up to go to the bathroom, and I watch his body move, struck by the interplay of muscles and the beautiful geometry it all creates. *Dancing is about creating lines,* I hear Laura say.

He leaves the door open to the bathroom, and I see him grab a vent brush and stand in front of the mirror, smoothing the waves of his hair as if he's getting ready for work.

"Did you really just comb your hair after sex?"

He flicks the light switch off in the bathroom. "I wanted to get rid of this flat pillow head."

He steps onto the raised platform of the futon and quickly burrows against me under the covers. "Let me give you a tour of the estate," he says, his breath on my ear. My eyes take in the one room that is this basement studio, the silver pipe running across the ceiling. "To the east there's my office. Farther down, the entertainment center. To the north, the kitchen, and, of course, the formal dining room." His voice, a fine imitation of a butler's. "And I believe you're already acquainted with the bedroom."

"Sir, what a view you have!" I point to the two-foot-by-two-foot window that provides the only daylight, looking out on an asphalt driveway covered in gray slush.

"You can't imagine what I pay for that," he says.

We fall back asleep; when I wake I have no idea whether it's day or night. Jet lag, the gray weather, and the dark apartment have stripped me of any sense of time. I do know that I'm hungry, however, so I crawl over him out of the bed, stopping to put my underwear back on before I forage in the refrigerator. I find Roman Meal bread, mayo, petrified iceberg lettuce, one slice of turkey, a dozen eggs, orange juice, and milk. Oh, and a yogurt. But it's strawberry. I don't like strawberry yogurt. Damn. I'm going to starve.

"Hey, you making something?" I hear the voice pipe up from the bed.

"It looks like the choice is eggs or eggs," I say. "You want some? Scrambled or over easy?"

"Do you know how to make egg salad?" he says, suddenly sounding all of about ten years old.

"Do *I* know how to make egg salad? Boy, I'll tell you what, that's like asking does a groundhog know dirt." My grandmother made the best egg salad in the history of the universe. (Considering that she's dead, I don't think she'll mind me spilling the secret: a pinch of tarragon and a splash of pickle juice.)

Twenty minutes later, a plate of egg salad sandwiches, cut in perfect triangles sans crust, is in front of him. He's now seated in the chair wearing a pair of striped boxers, watching the History Channel. With the hand that's not holding the TV remote he grabs a triangle and consumes half of it in one bite. "Wow," he says, "I knew this would happen someday."

How did a simple dance lead to this? I'm standing in a basement apartment in Queens, wearing nothing but blue underwear, the feel of this man still between my thighs.

And I have indeed just made him a sandwich.

All my girlfriends back in Los Angeles will say, "Did you have fun dancing?" The answer will be no, we didn't. I couldn't have picked a worse weekend to fly to New York. Another blizzard hits the city the evening after I get there, making anything but the most necessary travel impractical, if not impossible—especially for me, my blood made thin from so many years in California, the titanium rod in my leg aching like a giant metal tuning fork when struck by cold.

Still, I do have two meetings I must make, the supposed reasons for this whole excursion. So the next morning we are getting dressed together; he has a short workday at the studio and then rehearsals. The good thing about sharing a bathroom mirror with a short man is that I can put on my eye liner and he can shave without obstructing each other's view.

He assesses me after I get dressed. "You're not wearing enough. Layers. Put on another sweater. You're going to freeze." After I do he hands me a set of house keys on an enameled ring bearing the Cuban flag. "You'll get home before I do. If you lose these, you're dead." He then quizzes me on the train schedule, making sure I know which connections to take, and reviews contingency plans in case of mishaps.

"*Aye Papi*, I'm fine," I assure him in my best imitation of a Cuban accent, which isn't very good at all. Pathetic, in fact.

He rolls his eyes. "You got enough money?"

"Yeah."

He slaps me on the ass. "Good girl. *Vámanos*."

At the last minute he remembers the three weeks' worth of laundry he needs to drop off at the cleaners on the way to the subway. So here we are, trudging through snowdrifts the four long blocks to the station, me carrying a small laundry bag filled with underwear and socks, him toting a lawn-and-leaf-size garbage bag filled with clothes atop his head.

"Whoa! Watch the dog shit on the way back," he says. "You'll think it's frozen, but it's not. Trust me."

We walk in silence for another block. Snow sounds like glass being crunched under our boots, and our breath billows as curling white clouds in front of us. I've never understood how some of my friends on the East Coast claim to like winter, but in this moment I think maybe I see.

"Isn't this fun, baby?"

"It's sure all wine and roses with you," I say.

He smiles up at me from under his load. "Told you I'd show you a good time. You have to learn to listen to me."

Here's the part in the romantic comedy when the unlikely couple realizes they are actually in love, but then something happens that creates a misunderstanding, and it looks like they won't get together after all, yet, finally, in the last three minutes before she has to catch her plane back to L.A., everything is cleared up and, happily, they reconcile.

However, my life stubbornly refuses to fit into the three-act formula, so what we're actually looking at here is a man and a woman stuck in a studio apartment for two days as a blizzard rages, during which time they watch a lot of TV, eat egg salad sandwiches and even that horrible strawberry yogurt, have sex only one more time, sleep, lie next to each other on a futon, talk in the dark, and tell the truth.

I'm lying on my belly, hands folded over the thin pillow. "Did you see the way those people were looking at us on the subway? What the fuck was their problem?"

"They were wondering what a gorgeous redhead was doing with a punk-ass kid," he says.

"Shut up. The only one thinking that is you."

"Ah, *wrong*," he says. "I know for sure Angelo-the-Manager is thinking that."

Another day? Who can tell? Just voices in the dark.

"I want to fall in love and get married. Have someone real nice who will take care of my shit."

All at once I feel self-conscious; an uncomfortable sense comes over me like a chill. I can't put a name on what I feel right now, being here with him, what is between us, and for the first time that really bothers me. I turn my back to him and stare into the blackness.

"Hey." His foot pushes my leg. "What's wrong?"

"It's just weird, that's all." My voice is small. "Here I am with you, and I know you're not talking about me."

"Knock it off. You know you don't want to marry me. You don't feel for me that way." He pulls my shoulder so I'm lying on my back again. "You're big-time. Too big-time."

"And you're like community property. Nobody can put a copyright on you because you're in the public domain."

"What the fuck does that mean?"

"It's a metaphor, get it, about all your other women."

"Whatever. Anyhow, it's not love like that between us."

"It's some kind of love."

"Not that kind."

Finally I sigh. "We'd kill each other anyway."

He grabs my hand and brings it to his chest. "Friends?" he says.

I kiss his shoulder. "Friends," I agree.

We're silent for a moment. A snowy wind whips against the small window, and I think about how blue and clear it must be at home in Los Angeles, how much I'd like to be riding Harley.

"Baby, hey. You want to fuck now or what?" I can see the whiteness of his teeth as he smiles in the dark.

"Is Conan O'Brien on yet?"

He reaches over to the table for the TV remote. "Good call, baby, good call."

Holiday Schedule:
DanceLand will be closed
Dec. 18–Jan. 3.
Happy Holidays!

I n New York I managed to get one small magazine assignment and a miserable case of the flu, which I probably contracted on the flight home. (Planes, those flying incubators of bacteria and illness.) This means that I'm a snot-nosed, achy, exhausted, and feverish mess just in time for my mother to arrive for the Christmas holidays. What could be better? I ask.

It's the last Friday night before Christmas, and I am stuffed into a pair of black pantyhose and dance shoes, wearing a sequined skirt and a maroon scoop-neck top. Despite a double dose of flu medicine and a shower so steaming hot my skin is still pink, I feel like hell. I refuse, however, to miss this opportunity to take my mother to Sportsman's Lodge, for three excellent reasons.

1. They haven't got anything like this in Las Cruces, New Mexico, and I know she'll love watching the

dancers and hearing the band, even if she com-
plains the music is too loud.

2. I'm dying to know what she'll say seeing her
   klutzy, gawky daughter with the metal leg on a
   dance floor.

3. If we don't get out of the house, we'll be at each
   other's throats with Ginsu knives (yes, I own
   some) in another twenty-four hours.

"You look very lovely in your skirt, Miss Dunn," Mom
says as we enter the brightly lit ballroom, "but do you think
enough of your tits are showing in that top?"

"Who knows? I might get lucky," I snap at her before
literally gritting my teeth. I hold my breath for a second
before exhaling slowly. She stumbles then, slightly; I take her
arm to steady her, wrapping my fingers around the plush
sleeve of her emerald velvet pants suit. Her bright gold earrings match her gold necklace and metallic gold flats. I must
say gold looks beautiful next to her hair, which is growing in
again, a bit of curl appearing near the nape of her neck.

We find Laura's table, and while I make introductions I
catch Albert Torres's eye, the ask-me-to-dance-now-please!
expression on my face. Albert is a smart guy, and he quickly
comes to the table, which I adore him for. He's dressed
every inch the *patrón* tonight in a dark blue suit with a large
diamond stud in one ear. "Do you mind if I take your daughter for a dance?" he asks Mom. I can tell she's impressed by

the gentlemanly behavior because she simply smiles and nods, no wise-ass comment forthcoming.

"Albert," I whisper to him as we're heading toward the floor, "make me look good."

"Of course," he says, giving me a wink. "I already figured that one out."

The song is a Tito Puente classic, "Picadillo," a jazzy instrumental every salsa student has danced to at least once; in my case, about fifty times by this point, so I am familiar with when to expect the breaks and know the tempo well. Albert smoothly leads me into a series of simple single turns and a lovely back-spot turn, in which we whirl in a circle. I keep my eyes on his face, while around me spin bright colors and shapes, as if we have suddenly fallen into a kaleidoscope.

He holds me close for a moment. "I'm going to dip you at the end, so just trust me," he says.

I nod. The form of the dip is an exercise in surrender, your back arched, your pelvis forward, supported by a man's arms. This at once thrills and terrifies me.

And here comes the end of the song: he turns me for one spin, two spins, three spins—and just as I'm afraid I'll get off balance he pulls me into him, his arm on my back. I dramatically turn my face to the side and allow my body to relax as he bends forward, holding my weight.

We're both laughing as we stand upright. I hug him close. "I owe you for that, Albert."

"No problem," he says as he leads me back to Laura's table. "It's on the house."

When we return, Mom is clapping. "Excellent," she says, a smile still on her face.

Albert bows slightly and extends his hand to her. "May I have the pleasure?"

I press my lips together and look at her. Will she say yes? I imagine that she does, her long, curved nails touching his fingers, gracefully rising to her feet as if resurrected by the conga that's already beating the next number. Suddenly she is thirty years younger, her skin fleshy and warm, the rich flame of her hair like a cap of rubies over her head. Her hips move in a perfect figure eight, the promise that rings from the deep throatiness of her laughter turns every man's head.

But instead she is saying to Albert, "Gee, honey, thanks, but I banged up my damn knee on the trip over here and want to take it easy."

He nods politely and gives her a kind smile. As he straightens we catch each other's gaze. He spreads his broad hand over my shoulder and gives me an encouraging squeeze. "Have fun tonight, ladies."

Right after he leaves, Laura returns to the table and sits next to Mom. "Did you see your daughter dance?" asks Laura. "Aren't you proud? She's come a long way!"

"Yes." Mom nods grandly. "A chip off the old block."

I look at her, eyes rimmed with green liner and her mouth a circle drawn in lipstick the shade of ripe tomatoes. Mom, even now she exists in Technicolor.

I kiss her cheek. Soft hair covers her skin in a faint down, and her scent has the sweet bite of an after-dinner liqueur. "I hope so."

We're driving on the freeway back to my house, the hum of tires the only sound between us. I feel blurry and exhausted; am thinking only about curling up with a box of Kleenex and falling asleep. Then out of the silence I hear her say, "Armando really missed out."

"What?" I can't quite believe I heard her say that. She has never, ever uttered my father's name without prompting.

"I'm proud of you. That's all," she says. "It's his loss. But I can't say I didn't try to tell him."

I reach to touch her hand. "I know, Mom. Thank you."

"Did I ever tell you I even sent him letters in Italian?" She wraps her cool fingers through mine. "At the local high school there was this sweet old janitor from Italy. So after I, you know, found out, I went to him and his wife. I asked them to translate my letters into Italian so there'd be no way Armando wouldn't understand."

I can hardly speak. "No, you never told me."

"They were shocked, of course. Wanted him to do the honorable thing and come back to marry me. Well, we know how that turned out. Hey, how do I crack this window? I want to smoke."

I remove my hand from hers and push the button for the passenger-side window. The whine of the freeway cuts in. "How long did you wait for him to reply to your letters?"

The lighter briefly illuminates her profile. I see the cherry glow of her cigarette flare; then I'm hit with a wave of nicotine.

"Forever," she says finally. "I waited forever."

Christmas Eve. I'm buried under a mountain of covers until one o'clock in the afternoon, when I hear the phone ring.

"Mom!" I croak. "Can you get that, please? Mom?"

She must be downstairs having a cup of coffee with Nacha in the kitchen, or eating lunch. Either way it means I have to rouse myself out of bed and pick up the phone in the other room.

I pick up the receiver with a raspy "Hello?"

"Sam, is that you? It's Carol, I'm calling from the barn." Carol and I are friendly, but we're not friends. I get a queasy feeling in my gut.

"Yes, hi, what's up?"

"It's Harley, he seems sick—"

I'm at once awake, already starting to pull off my pajama bottoms and search for a pair of jeans. "Give me twenty minutes."

"It might just be a light colic, nothing serious." She is trying to sound reassuring.

"I'll be right there."

"I'd call the vet—"

"Thanks, Carol." I don't think I wait to say good-bye, already searching my phone book for the veterinarian's number.

Colic for a horse is more than the tummy upset it can be in humans; the complicated pattern of the equine digestive track means colic can make a horse uncomfortable for a few hours, or it can lead to a ruptured intestine, an agonizing death. That's the terror of colic for a horse owner: it comes on fast, caused by a dozen possible reasons, and you never know how severe it will get.

I saw Harley just yesterday, and he was happy and relaxed, cozied up next to his stable mate, an old Palomino aptly named Buddha. I'd just jumped on bareback to meander around the stable for a little bit, too worn out from the flu to do anything else. I can't quite believe there's anything really wrong; Harley looked so good such a short time ago. Still, you never want to take the risk.

I get the answering machine at the vet's. Of course this has to be Christmas Eve. I dial the answering service, explaining I have an emergency. Both my regular vets are off for the holidays; I tell the operator I'll take anybody with a vet license.

I am still pulling on my jacket when I get downstairs, going out the back door through the kitchen.

Mom sits at the wooden table, coffee mug in hand. "She

lives! I thought you'd never wake up—wait, where are you going?"

"Harley."

"Hold on, for chrissakes. I'm coming with you."

The December sky is the color of dishwater, and a mean wind blows off the Pacific. My cell phone keeps ringing; I hope it's the vet telling me not to worry, but all the calls are from people at the barn, all giving the same message: hurry. Finally I turn it off.

I know the route to the barn so well I could probably drive it blindfolded, but I'm gripping the steering wheel hard enough for my hands to start to ache. My mother turns toward me to speak and I think she's about to warn me to slow down, but instead she says, "We're almost there, right?"

We come to the canyon, the steep scissor cliffs looking not any different from the first time I saw them seven years ago, on that trail ride with Harley that led to my accident. Kate and Edward's barn stands at the base, before the canyon opens into state park lands.

Just as the car crests the ridge on the final descent into the barn's parking lot, the clouds open up and a cold rain starts to pour. I wish I were making this up. I wish it were just a good storytelling technique to add tension and fore-shadow events to come, but the fact is that the goddamn rain really does fall precisely at this moment, and in the very next instant I really do see my beautiful horse—the being who has been my companion, my secret keeper, my guru showing me the way to a better life, and, most of all my love, my absolute love—I see him collapse in the wet earth.

Many things happen.

Daniel, the horse trainer named Tim, Carol, two stable hands, a young woman with a long blond ponytail who is a vet just out of school, and I, we all try to get Harley back on his feet, pulling on his halter and prodding, yelling, pleading, coaxing. He flails and struggles, at one point coming up for just a moment. But his legs jut out strangely, and he looks bewildered that he cannot control them, his head jerking around at a sickening angle before his massive weight crashes down again in what is now the soupy mud of the stable area.

I have a vague sense of the vet telling me she is doing everything she can, that she has given him all the necessary medication for colic but it seems to be some kind of neurological condition. Perhaps he has a brain tumor, or some rare virus that had no obvious symptoms to signal a progression into something serious. She has put a catheter in his neck to pipe fluids and pain medication into his system. "All we can do now is wait a few hours and see if he gets up," she says. "I have another call to get to, but please page me if there is any more I can do. Good luck."

I am sitting in the mud with Harley's great head in my lap, unaware that my clothes are plastered to my skin, my jacket over his steaming neck as others cover his hot, sweating body with blankets to protect him from the rain and a chill. *What the fuck do you know, stupid Barbie? Can't you see this horse is perfect? Get something out of your bag and make him well! Where did you get your DVM, by mail order?* I think I just nod.

Meanwhile, Tim and Daniel bark orders, instructing the stable hands how to build a makeshift tent around us using a series of tarps and ropes. One of the men comes with a large load of wood shavings to spread as dry cover over the ground. Just then, Harley suddenly whips his head up, thrashing his legs before him in an effort to pull himself up.

"Sam! Get out of the way!" I hear Mom's voice rise above the others as I roll from him. I know everyone is sure those hooves will strike out like a weapon and I will be hit again, but somehow I know I won't be. Not this time.

Harley tries, but he cannot lift his own weight. In the process of his struggle the catheter pulls out of his neck, the tubing springs out as he begins to bleed.

"Shit shit shit shit shit," I say, my hands shaking as I grab for the catheter and tubing, tears making my sight nothing more than a smeared blur.

"Get out of the way." Mom is there beside me, taking the catheter from my hands. She hasn't been this close to a horse in years, preferring to watch from a comfortable distance, or pet them lightly on the nose. If Harley should strike out to try to rise again, she won't be able to move fast enough to get out of the way. I feel real fear at the thought of that.

"No, it's not safe—"

"Just shut up and move so I can get in there." I hear in her voice the nurse she has been throughout more than three decades, the voice of operating rooms and countless life-threatening emergencies. Her hands don't even tremble as she quickly reinserts the catheter and starts the IV once more. Harley groans.

"There," she says, and only now do I detect a faint quiver in her voice, breathlessness, and no doubt some exhaustion. She is scared and wet and miserable with cold, but she has done this for me, because this horse is what I love in the world. In this moment I feel a well of regret fill within me, the space I have held for resentment and judgment of her that I had thought was fathomless.

Tim, the horse trainer, tells me I should take Mom home and get into some dry clothes myself. "We'll take care of him while you're gone, don't worry," says this usually taciturn cowboy. "It won't be much good if you get pneumonia."

I whisper in Harley's ear, telling him I'll be back soon, and not to try to get up unless I'm there. You may think it's crazy, but he listens to me.

I don't remember much of what happens on the drive, but I do know I only take five minutes to towel off and get into dry clothes. Still, the trip there and back takes a full hour, the storm making the road slow going.

I return to see the glow of many flashlights coming from the makeshift tent, a group surrounding the massive form of my fallen horse. A new truck is in the driveway. Tim called Dr. Sullivan, an experienced, well-known vet in the area. I feel a rush of hope—now here's someone who will know what to do. He'll have answers. Everything will be fine.

But when I get to the tent, all the faces are somber. Some avert their gazes. Kate, Edward, and their daughter, Thaïs, are there too, and they turn to me with a look of so much caring that I want to run away, I want to scream and tell everyone there is some terrible mistake.

I see Dr. Sullivan checking Harley's chest, his breaths labored and heavy, and I rush to kneel at his head. If I could only describe the impossible depths of those huge eyes, the soft flutter of his lids. But his ears are twitching weirdly, a movement I have never seen, and then I think of the strange little twitch of his muzzle that I had only ever thought was a charming personality quirk. Then the way he had recently started to suddenly fall asleep on his feet, a sort of equine narcolepsy. I thought he was at age seventeen just finally slowing down. Perhaps there had been signs. I just couldn't read them.

Dr. Sullivan is saying, "I'm sorry, Miss Dunn—"

"What if money were no object?" What would I give to keep this love? Anything. More than what I have. I will borrow, steal. "What could we do?"

"If this horse were Sea Biscuit, we could fly him to the clinic and keep him alive just long enough to figure out what's killing him. It's something neurological, but what, exactly, we can't say for sure without more tests."

"So there's nothing else to be done? Nothing? Nothing on the entire fucking planet?"

The vet shakes his head and looks at me in a way that brooks no further discussion.

Maybe that's when I start to sob, or maybe it's when the vet brings out the giant syringe that I know he will use to tap the lethal injection through the same catheter my mother so careful placed.

As Dr. Sullivan is making the preparations I run my hands over the crescent of Harley's jaw, kissing the soft velvet of his muzzle, thanking him for being in my life all these years. He's quiet, his eyes half closed, the full weight of his head in my lap.

"*Tómalo,* Sammy." Daniel stands at my side, handing me a large mug from which to drink. I shake my head, but he tells me again to drink, so I take the mug and feel the sting of mescal down my throat. Warmth spreads within me instantly as if a small campfire has just been lit.

"Ready?" Dr. Sullivan asks.

No, I could never be ready. But I nod my head. Harley stiffens his neck for a moment, and then he lets out a long sigh. His eyelids flutter once, then no more. I cup my hand over his eye, curling myself around the long sculpture of his head.

Then I hear what sounds like a giant oak being uprooted and split in two, as if struck by a bolt of lightning.

I look up and become aware that the inside of the tent is completely silent except for a gasping, hopeless wail, a keening too awful to describe. But no one moves. No one speaks. Things are as they were just seconds ago. I know then that must have been the sound of my own heart struck by one tremendous jolt of grief, which seems to flow and gain energy from all that came before it, over years and years, over lifetimes.

The head of he whom I have loved most truly and most dear weighs heavily against my legs. I bend myself even closer around him, but no breath comes from that velvet nose.

A feeling of ash is all that remains.

I get back to the house, but when? I have no idea. I don't feel my legs as they walk up the stairs.

Mom sits on my couch reading a book, a pair of reading glasses perched on her nose. She looks up when I enter the room.

"Edward called and told me." She opens her arms. "My poor baby."

I fall into her then, crushing my face against her chest, my arms wrapped around her as if I were no older than two. "Oh Mom," I repeat over and over until I lose track of the words.

She holds me tight and does not tell me to stop crying.

Salsa IV

Terrific variety of step patterns, stylish footwork, intricate turns, and cool timings to play with. Must be a student for at least six months. Class ongoing.

I want to believe that, if left to our own devices when we are ill or wounded, we human things gravitate toward the perfect sources of healing for our particular pain. This, maybe, is not true. I have no evidence apart from my own experience to support such a statement. But I like the idea, so I am taking it as a personal fact. Says me, again.

Take dancing as an example. Researchers at Cornell University spent money to verify what anybody who listens to pop music on the radio already knows: music with rapid tempos played in major keys correlates to happiness. Other studies have proven that being touched stimulates the immune system and raises serotonin levels, the happiness chemical of the brain, to put the most complicated psychiatry in gross layman terms. And eye contact stimulates the release of oxytocin, one of the central chemicals involved in love and attachment. All this is going on during one three-minute mambo.

I must earn some money during this time, because nobody has repossessed my car for nonpayment. I must eat something during this time, because nobody puts me in a hospital. I must bathe; I must answer phone calls; I must walk the dog. I don't recall doing any of it.

I experience life in the wake of Harley's death as one long nighttime spent under club lights, the imprint of a hundred fingers pressing onto my skin, my feet becoming callused and toughened, my hair turning a shade lighter, leeched of color from the heavy salt of my own sweat.

In my mind's eye I replay again and again a fantasy about what my Carlos Gomez will be when I meet him. Because this is fantasy, not only is my Carlos Gomez physically beautiful and brilliant in an artistic kind of way, but he loves and adores me like only horses and dogs do in real life. In my mind, I am completely content in my love for him, and I am true and good-natured as any heroine should be. And in this fantasy, my Carlos Gomez is mute, so that these pictures run as a silent movie through my mind. Perhaps he is deaf as well, so the ways we know each other are wordless and physical, which seem to me to be the truest ways to know anything or anyone.

Words are as vast as stars in number, languages are kinds of constellations. Despite their limitlessness, the ones that yield perfect expression are rare. Even when you do find them, that perfection is transient. See the ridiculousness of what I'm doing? Trying to describe why description is fruitless. Things move, feelings change, thoughts evolve, yet words mean to fix them permanently in a shape, as amber would a fly.

Actions just are. You cry; a shoulder is there. You laugh; other laughter joins you. You feel cold in the night; an arm wraps around your waist and pulls you into the warmth of his sleeping body. Only through this, the most trusted form of knowing.

Here we are, the Friday before Valentine's Day at Sportsman's Lodge. I have locked eyes across the ballroom with one of the Brahmins; let's say he's from San Salvador, magnetically sexy in a tortured poet kind of way. We've been seriously flirting for about a week now. He asked me to dance back in November, but I whacked him in another of my combat salsa maneuvers, so he has been skittish about asking me again. I haven't belted anyone for a month, and I'm plotting how I can shimmy with him one more time.

Now I wish I could reach back and slap myself and say "leave well enough alone," because, despite the fact that

I fall deeply in love with him after a to-die-for first date, where he kisses me on the Ferris wheel at the Santa Monica Pier, this tortured El Salvadorian poet doesn't want the Carlos Gomez job. In fact, I'm going to end up sniveling about this one for so long after he dumps me that even J. tells me to shut up about it already. *Que será, será* and all that. Just let me say, though, that while he's listing the reasons he wants to break up with me, he mentions in passing that "he never likes to date other dancers," which means of course he considers me a dancer. This fact makes me so happy that for a second I don't know whether to smile, or to cry about the fact he is dumping me. The crying wins, ultimately.

But none of this happens until months after tonight. Sorry, as usual, I've gotten way ahead of myself.

Anyway, my tortured El Salvadorian poet gets pulled onto the dance floor by one of the zillions of women who want a great lead, so I settle myself on a chair at Laura's table.

I'm going to say the band tonight is Johnny Polanco y Sus Amistads, because it usually is. Laura, in a zebra-print off-the-shoulder top, is dancing with a young man who is trying desperately to impress the diva with his cha-cha-cha. I can see by the polite smile on her face it's not working. Clelia and Veronica are sitting on the other side of the table, heads bowed together, deep in another discussion. Errol is dancing off to the side with Sonia, the two gliding in synch to this famous cha-cha, "Salchicha Con Huevos," literally translated as "sausage and eggs," but I'm pretty sure the lyrics have nothing to do with breakfast.

As the song ends, dancers with skins shiny and glowing spill off the dance floor, a flush of color and movement like silver-scaled fish escaping from a net. It surprises me to suddenly realize that I know by name, by sight, or have danced with, nearly every one of these people, this village of salsa lovers to which I now belong. At this same time last year, they were all strangers. Which reminds me, I have to call New York tomorrow and sing "Happy Birthday"/"Feliz Cumpleaños" to you-know-who. February 15, his birthday, my salsa anniversary.

Jacob stands in front of me. "Why so quiet tonight?"

I shrug and smile up at him. "No reason. Just thinking."

I go back to drinking my Shirley Temple, wondering if I have any moleskin pads in my purse to cushion the toe on these new shoes. All of $150, and they're burning the skin off my toes, thank you very much. I find two packs of breath mints (a standard courtesy in the dance world), a small bottle of baby powder (a little sprinkle cures a sticky floor), and hand lotion (self-evident), but no moleskin. Guess I'm going to have blisters.

I feel a tap on my shoulder. Jacob stands with his hand outstretched.

Me?

Did I, somewhere, somehow, pass the invisible threshold into the realm of serious dancer?

"Yes?" I say, hesitantly.

"Do you merengue?" he asks.

"You could say I have some experience with meren-gue." I can't help but smile.

"Come on, kiddo," he tells me, taking my hand, leading me into what I take as my official graduation dance. "This is a nice one."

It's like that. Go ahead and try to anticipate the signs, but you never really know when the turns are going to happen. You just have to wait for the lead.

Shines

Learn show-stopping solo footwork like the
reverse grapevine hook flick from our all-star
instructors:

Being a strong dancer independently makes
for better partnering!
Must be intermediate level or above. See
front desk for details.

Tempe is his name. He's not my usual type. There
are all kinds of things wrong with him.

For starters, I've never really liked quarter
horses. He's shorter than Harley by a full hand, and while
he's very muscular now, as he gets older he'll probably
have a weight problem. Plus, he's been known to buck and

spin like a rodeo bronco. He's a paint with large splashes of white over a sorrel coat and a black mane and tail, which is not a coloring I'm partial to. Still, he's flashy and a rascal. He steals things out of my jean pockets and is a genius at picking the lock on his corral with that rubber nose, pink as a pencil eraser. It took me a while to want to be near a barn again, and I started riding him only as a favor to his owner, but now it's become a regular thing. No promises. I haven't bought him or anything. I'm just riding. But we get along, Tempe and I. What can I say? Bad boys like me.

Speaking of bad boys, I e-mailed Rafael after Harley died to tell him the news. Eight years of shoeing that horse, and he didn't even send a condolence card. Go figure.

Mom now contends that she never really liked him anyway. Apart from this selective memory loss, she's the same as ever. Even has a "friend" I'll call Dilbert whom she met in the trailer—excuse me—mobile home—excuse me—*manufactured housing park*, a guy who makes her drink protein shakes for her health and sometimes takes her to the horse races up in Ruidoso, New Mexico.

Ironic, isn't it? My sixty-something mother seems to have landed a Carlos Gomez without stepping a foot outside the porch on her doublewide, while her daughter, living *la vida loca* in exciting Los Angeles, can't seem to find a man who'll spring for a latte at Starbucks, let alone customblend a protein drink. Yet I've acquired a boundless faith that there is a Carlos Gomez somewhere in the world. Someday

I'll be ready to see him, and I'm just going to walk around a corner and there he'll be. I expect he'll say, "What took you so long?" or maybe he'll say it like, *"¿Por qué te tardastes tanto?"* Or, maybe, he'll say nothing at all.

This uncharacteristic faith might be a product of knowing at least two dozen men who have never and will never drop me when I'm in their arms. You could say my dance partners are teaching me to trust, three minutes at a time.

I've been thinking a lot about this. By now I've asked a lot of people how they came to salsa, and invariably the story is somehow linked to love, lost or found or hoped for. There have been moments when I have walked off a dance floor and caught the eye of onlookers, their faces bright with the same breathless anticipation, the same excitement I still feel at the dance, and I know that inside them a hunger has been sparked for something they can't yet name. It seems to me that everyone at some time searches for their own version of a Carlos Gomez. But when we find him, or her, what do we want that to mean, really? I have felt this in my body; I have seen this with my eyes: all we ever actually desire is the experience of being well and truly *alive*.

Which is to say, yes, I still dance just as much, if not more. Remember those antidrug films from high school, how they lectured that one toke off a spliff would lead straight down the road to shooting heroin, free-basing cocaine? Salsa is like that. Now that I've started, I've been dabbling in *rumba, bachata* . . . I've had an offer for West Coast swing, so I'm thinking, *What have I got to lose?* My dance addiction hasn't yet gone as far as the sadistically compelling Argentinean *tango* (God help you, Robert Duvall), but I'm not making any promises. Anything can happen when you start to dance, and does. For instance, who'd have thought J.'s husband would decide to take lessons with Laura? Truly, it doesn't matter if he learns or not; J.'s just happy he's trying, that after all these years he still desires to be the only one to hold her in his arms.

And who'd have thought that a five-foot-four-on-a-tall-day Cuban Gene Kelly Casanova ex-lover would end up as one of my beloved male friends? I sometimes still sleep on his futon when I go to New York—no, not what you think. He's got his own bed in a nice two-bedroom apartment, befitting his status as director of a great dance studio in SoHo. He's got a little more gray in his hair, too, but it suits him. He did indeed put some big things together.

I still love dancing with him, and do it whenever I get the chance, like a couple of weeks ago when he was out here over the Labor Day weekend to lead a series of workshops. I was conscripted for the assignment of giving him a ride to the airport when the last workshop was done. In fairness I was the logical choice for chauffeur, seeing as I don't have a regular day job at the moment. I think I forgot to mention that the New York magazine canned me as a correspondent after I'd pitched my fifteenth salsa story idea. But everything worked out fine. It gave me time to write a book.

"Babe, do I get any royalties on this book, by the way?" he asks as we're driving on the 405, heading to the airport.

"What are you talking about?" I have to turn the radio down to hear this one.

"But I'm the one who gave you the sandwich line," he says.

"Yeah, but you didn't *know* you were giving me the sandwich line. You were just asking for a sandwich in a particularly interesting context."

"Typical," he says. "You're going to take all the money, get all the credit, and the guy in the story—meaning *me*, thank you—is going to look like a fucking moron. And, besides, you never made me a sandwich."

He astounds me.

"How can you say that?" I whack him on the shoulder. "'Oh, babe, this is the best egg salad sandwich I've ever had.' 'Oh, babe, can you make another egg salad?' Queens, blizzard, remember? That was me."

"Oh, yeah, that's right," he says, putting his hands up in surrender. "Chill, OK? I'm sorry, OK? Now I remember."

I push the volume button on the radio, and we drive for another couple of minutes with the tinny ring of Madonna's "Borderline" in the speakers. Finally the top of my head explodes.

"I can't believe you forgot those egg salad sandwiches!!!"

He turns his black-fringed eyes, those wells of sincerity, to look at me. "Baby, you have to understand. I eat a lot of sandwiches."

Gratitude

Carlos Gomez, thank you for being such a great sport. Many blessings to you and yours. Jennifer Barth talked me into this, and I will be forever beholden. It's a joy working with you. Thanks to Sam Douglas and the rest of the staff at Henry Holt. Peter Matson, I'll fly across the country to have lunch with you anytime.

Brilliant pals and partners in crime: Julianne Ortale and Rachel Resnick, I adore you both. I deeply appreciate the support and great ideas from mentor and friend Lee K. Abbott. Thanks James Miller, just because. Darin Strauss and Noah Blake, I will always take your suggestions. Michael Datcher, Mary Rakow, Lola Willoughby, Beverly Olevin, Janet Fitch, Bruce Bauman, Cathryn Michon, and Sandra Tsing Loh: thanks for reading along the way. Bob and Peg Boyers, Marc Woodworth, and Don McCormack of the New York State Summer Writers Institute: thank you, as always, for the support and encouragement. William and Dana Kennedy, you're inspirations for dancing, writing, partnering, eating, living.

Linda Venis and the rest of the staff at the UCLA Extension Writers Program, I deeply appreciate everything you do. Thanks too to my workshop participants, who always teach me a thing or two. Lauren Tom, Shannon Morris, Karmen Klegoe, and Alex Shaffer, you are treasures.

My salsa family, I'm lucky to have found all of you:

Laura Canellias really is a goddess, and Albert Torres is the reason so many thousands know the rapture of this dance. I vow my eternal loyalty.

Clelia Rodriguez and Veronica Zarate, Beige James and Sonia Gonzales, you are dear *comadres*.

Fernando Barrera and Dave Burke, you're like the big brothers I wish I'd grown up with.

Dreamboats on the dance floor: Mike Bello, Sir Harry Bowens, Jerry Gabaldon, Dario Gonzalez, Daniel Klein, Craig Morris, and, of course, Raul Santiago, your careful explanations and urgings to dance are priceless.

Josie Brava Martinez, Olivia Dasso, Faith Ernest, and Chantal Saguespe are among the many stunning *salseras* who embody the ideal all would-be dancers like me work toward.

Alan Geik of Alma Del Barrio (that's 88.9 FM on your radio dial, Los Angeles): a million thanks for sharing your time and vast knowledge of this music and its history. Joe Cassini, thank you as well for generously educating me.

Much gratefulness goes to my long-suffering regular partners in the clubs, who dance with me even though I have often stepped on their toes and clobbered them with my elbow, without whom I would have given up quicker than I started. It's ironic that I don't know most of your last names, considering that we've sweated together so often: Alan Feuerstein, Alvin, Art, Don Johnson, Jesus Moreno, Carlos, Enrique, Luis, Freslit LaFrance, Sidney James, Jerry, Jeff, Phil, and, above all, Errol.

Raymunda de la Cruz, muchisimas gracias por todo, por su amor y su consejo. Usted es mi angelita de la guarda. Daniel, gracias por ayudarme y por cuidar de mi caballo. Thanks, Jordan Cohen, John Buksbazen, and Erika Richardson for keeping me on track. The Albert family, my appreciation and affection are greater than I can express.

Mom, my muse, I love you so very much.

¡Ya bailamos!

About the Author

SAMANTHA DUNN is the author of *Not By Accident: Reconstructing a Careless Life* and the novel *Failing Paris*, which was a finalist for the PEN/West award. Her writing has appeared in the *Los Angeles Times*, *In Style*, *O Magazine*, *Ms.*, and numerous other national publications. She lives in Southern California.

Questions for Discussion

1. Does Samantha's aversion to dancing stem from her mother's proficiency? How does this resistance fuel her approach to learning salsa?

2. Samantha hopes that through dance lessons she will find the way to develop a meaningful relationship with a person rather than with her horse. She comes to realize that dance class is a way for people to connect; discuss the ways salsa provides a chance to break free of the "quiet desperation" of loneliness.

3. Discuss the exhilaration Samantha feels at this attempt at grace since she has always been such a tomboy.

4. Samantha feels a sense of being untethered; how does this state of mind contribute to her decision to learn to dance salsa? Why does Samantha's instructor tell her "you don't need a reason to dance"?

5. Describe the moment at the Conga Room when Samantha has her epiphany.

6. Discuss the three stepping stones on the path that leads to spiritual mastery and how it relates to learning to dance: great doubt, great faith, and great persistence.

7. Laura, Samantha's teacher, promises grace, coordination, and partnership. Is Samantha able to accomplish these goals?

8. Salsa is a way to act out one's own sensuality in a safe way with another person. Is salsa dancing just extended foreplay? How does one avoid making the mistake of confusing the dancer with the person? What are the sexual politics of salsa?

9. Discuss the nonverbal communication of dance— dance as a physical language.

10. How does Samantha's dedication to salsa affect and perhaps alter her relationship with her mother?

11. How does Samantha apply her principle of faith in Carlos Gomez to her life?